G R E E N L A N D

ELLESMERE
ISLAND

Thule

Atlantic Ocean

Baffin Bay

Grise Fjord

DEVON
ISLAND

Lancaster Sound

SOMERSET
ISLAND

BAFFIN ISLAND

CTORIA ISLAND

Hudson Strait

Wager Bay

Bathurst
Inlet

NEWFOUNDLAND

SOUTHAMPTON
ISLAND

COATS
ISLAND

NORTHWEST
TERRITORIES

Hudson Bay

Q U E B E C

*Great
Slave
Lake*

*Gulf of
St.Lawrence*

CAPE CHURCHILL

CHURCHILL

*James
Bay*

NEW
BRUNSWICK

*Churchill
River*

*Lake
Athabasca*

*Reindeer
Lake*

*Lynn
Lake*

Nelson River

ALBERTA SASKATCHEWAN

M A N I T O B A

O N T A R I O

ARCTIC CIRCLE

POLAR DANCE
BORN OF THE NORTH WIND

Tom Mangelsen 12/96

PHOTOGRAPHS BY THOMAS D. MANGELSEN
STORY BY FRED BRUEMMER

DESIGN BY LEE CARLMAN RIDDELL   TEXT EDITED BY CARA BLESSLEY   PUBLISHED BY IMAGES OF NATURE

Special Edition

Photographs copyright by Thomas D. Mangelsen

Text copyright by Fred Bruemmer

Illustrations copyright by Mike Reagan

Design by Lee Carlman Riddell

Editing by Cara Blessley

Production coordination by Steven Goff

Printed in Hong Kong through Palace Press International, San Francisco

Images of Nature® is a federally registered trademark of Thomas D. Mangelsen, Inc., Omaha, Nebraska.

For information about reproduction rights to the photographs in this book

or inquiries about limited edition prints, contact:

Images of Nature®, Post Office Box 37429, 13303 "F" Street, Omaha, Nebraska 68137.

Telephone 1-800-228-9686   Facsimile 1-800-832-4571

http://www.mangelsen.com

ISBN 0-9633080-8-4

TO THE MEMORY OF MY FATHER AND MOTHER

AND TO

MY BROTHERS

HAL, DAVID, AND BILL

FOREWORD

I have known Tom and his photography for nearly twenty years. Each time I see one of his new images I wonder, as do many others, how can he do it? He's admired not only for the quality of his photographs but also for the quantity of outstanding images. Each time I gaze at one of his photos I am amazed at its naturalness; the wildlife subject is just where it should be, but how did Tom get it there? Not by coercion, not by stalking, but more often by patience: long, cold waits, cramped muscles and a sense of timing. Taking one outstanding photograph is difficult; taking so many, especially in the arctic conditions of wind and cold, is extraordinary. Seeing the starkly beautiful image "Born Of The North Wind" for the first time impressed me even more than my own first sighting of a polar bear almost thirty years ago. ❖ In 1967 I had gone north to James Bay, Manitoba, in hopes of observing polar bears. This trip was in part research, but also personal. I wanted to compare the habits of polar bears with those of the grizzly and black bears I knew from Yellowstone. Between 1959 and 1971, working with my brother John, I had conducted research on a population of grizzlies in Yellowstone National Park. I had also observed the interaction of grizzlies with black bears, and as my admiration and respect for bears grew, I wanted to know more about other species of bear. ❖ Grizzly bears live in a relatively confined area, and I was curious to see how a bear would live in the unlimited space of the north. How would a bear's behavior change if it didn't sleep through the winter? Would specializing in one food source make the polar bear's senses and hunting skills sharper? Would the bears somehow gather to socialize? ❖ I was told I would only see a glimpse of the polar bears—if at all—but hoped it would at least give me a sense of what their world was like. I knew it would take a lifetime of study to answer all my questions. ❖ Tom Mangelsen's photographs have brought most of the arctic world of the polar bear to light. You can be sure that Tom's bear images and other arctic photographs in this book accurately portray the mood of the polar bear and its world. Tom has captured the unique character of the polar bear. ❖ Fred Bruemmer, with his years of arctic experience and his knowledge of polar bears, superbly complements Tom's images. While Tom stimulates the mind with frames of arctic light, Fred Bruemmer blends the lore and natural history of the polar bear into his creative story. His words are the reflections of countless hours spent on the ice with the bears, watching and learning. I can't think of any more qualified collaborators than Tom Mangelsen and Fred Bruemmer to bring the polar bear to life in a book.

FRANK CRAIGHEAD

PREFACE

The morning awakens to the song of the hermit thrush. There is no other song, not even that of the loon, that brings me back to the north country quite like the serene, flutelike call of the hermit thrush. In early June, the song begins at daybreak and continues 'til mid-morning, picking up again in late afternoon; at this latitude, the thrush sings until darkness falls at midnight. ❖ Most of the ice went out on Reindeer Lake this past week—far out in the middle large pans of rotten ice remain. The breeze switches, coming off the ice, and the temperature in the black spruce, birch, and alder forest where I sit changes dramatically. ❖ Gulls wheel above the islands in Lawrence Bay and a bald eagle clutching a small lake trout heads toward its giant nest in an ancient birch, now leafless and dying after being scorched by one of last summer's forest fires. ❖ Looking northeast toward the ice, I think of last summer on the tundra along the west shore of Hudson Bay. Much of the north was on fire. Smoke shrouded the midnight sun. Hudson Bay ice was breaking up and pods of beluga whales moved into the Churchill River. Flocks of eiders courted among the ice floes, black guillemots and red-breasted mergansers swung low over Cape Merry. ❖ It was my tenth season on Hudson Bay and possibly my thirtieth visit to the Far North: from the Yukon-Kuskokwim deltas in Alaska, east to Hudson and Wager Bays, north to Ellesmere and Baffin Islands in Canada's Northwest Territories. My earliest trips were mostly for birds, my more recent ones for polar bears. I saw my first polar bear tracks in May, 1977, along the ice edge three miles west of Point Barrow, Alaska. It would be almost ten years later before I saw my first polar bear on Hudson Bay near Churchill, Manitoba. ❖ In some ways this book is a culmination of those experiences, a love affair with the Far North and a passion for polar bears. The same day I saw my first polar bear I met Fred Bruemmer, someone I had known only through books and articles about the Arctic. Nearly every fall season since then, we have spent countless hours along the western shore of Hudson Bay observing, photographing, and enjoying polar bears together. ❖ By 1996 I had amassed some 85,000 images of polar bears and associated arctic wildlife. My passion had run amok. It was time to do a book and I knew no one more gifted to write it than Fred. ❖ With the number of books on polar bears already in print, including one of Fred's own, the challenge was how to do a book differently than had been done before. From the beginning we agreed that it would be neither advantageous, nor for that matter, possible, for us to attempt to illustrate the others' vision of the Arctic. ❖ Fred has written a story about polar bears and the land where they live, based on his many years of observation, scientific knowledge, and experience living in the Arctic. I wanted to make images of bears in the northern landscape that showed not only close up views but large, expansive ones. In some cases, the images illustrate specific passages in the text; others are merely representative of the animal or bird or the landform. I wanted to capture the essence of the polar bear and the Arctic in its many moods, textures, and seasons. ❖ Although all the pictures were taken in the Arctic, not all were taken at the same location as a passage in the text or necessarily at the same time of year. Our common goal was to celebrate in words and in pictures an unforgettable image of polar bears and the Far North.

TDM   JUNE 7, 1996, REINDEER LAKE, SASKATCHEWAN

ACKNOWLEDGMENTS

My sincere thanks and deepest appreciation:

To Fred Bruemmer for writing a beautiful story, for the inspiration you have given me, and for all the fun times and experiences we've shared watching polar bears. To Maud Bruemmer for encouraging Fred in all that he does. ❖ To Cara Blessley, my partner, for caring and giving so much to this project, and for help and support on the tundra. For all the birds and bears we've shared, and for editing the text. ❖ To Lee Carlman Riddell for designing the book, and for making it all work. For the understanding of a common goal, for the enthusiasm and unending patience after long hours spent at the light table or computer, and for respecting last minute wishes or changes with a smile. And, to Ed Riddell for his critical eye and creative input. ❖ To Mike Reagan for painting the beautiful map. ❖ To Frank, Shirley, and Charlie Craighead for your enduring friendship, valuable suggestions and kind words. The bears could not have better friends nor could I. ❖ To Cliff Kirkpatrick, Kerry Lamb, Jeffrey Williamson, Mindy Breen Mitchell, Mikelle Schlupp, Samantha Stout, and Susan Carlman who gave much needed assistance. ❖ To Steven Goff and Mandy Stier for their encouragement, enthusiasm and contribution in coordinating the production of the book. And to Heather Bennett, Peter Stougaard, Rick Smolan, Ken Coburn, and Donna and Webb Blessley for valuable input and suggestions. ❖ To Karla Swiggum who had the daunting task of cataloging the thousands of transparencies; for the enduring patience over many months as I edited and re-edited. To Victoria Blumberg, for all the help and cheerful attitude when it was most needed. ❖ To the special friends who shared the experience and who assisted in valuable ways, especially Dan and Marcia Guravich, Len and Bev Smith, Steve Miller, Rob Watson, Charlie King, Dennis Compayre, Kevin Burke and Brian Ladoon; and to Jo Brink, Kathy Watkins, John Pitcher, Cynthia Thieriot, Dave Myers, Tina Dalton, Chip Houseman, and Greg Winston. ❖ To Hal, David, and Bill for being the best of brothers. ❖ To my treasured friends Spence Wilson, and Glenn and Beth Exum, for the special ways they have contributed to my life. ❖ To all the scientists who work with bears, especially Chuck Jonkel, Ian Stirling, and Thor Larsen, and to the painters whose work has inspired me, especially Robert Bateman, Bob Kuhn and Andrew Wyeth. ❖ To the memory of Michio Hoshino, whose friendship and photography I will always cherish. ❖ To my friends and associates at Images of Nature for giving me the time and support to complete such a large project, especially Mary Rommelfanger, and Carl and Georgia Gruenler. To Dan Fulton, Mike Campisi, Todd Robinson, Michael Miratsky, Keith Bronstein, David Gautereaux, Gary Lortz, and Tom and Linda Hunter. ❖ To my mother and all the sleepless nights when she said, "Tom, stay away from those damn bears," and with a know-better motherly smile, "Just please be careful." ❖ To the bears and all the wildlife for tolerating my presence in their land and for adding so much to my life. May there be many fat seals for the bears, and may the seals, for their sake, be wary and slippery.

TDM

TABLE OF CONTENTS

PATH OF THE AURORA

The land to the west of Hudson Bay is at once ancient, and new. Part of Canada's Precambrian Shield, rent and riven by ice and age, is 3.6 billion years old, among the oldest on earth. For millions of years advancing and retreating ice caps and glaciers have scoured these ancient rocks and scooped out depressions now filled by myriad lakes. ❖ Ten thousand years ago, when humans built their first cities in the Middle East and hunter-gatherers became pastoralists or farmers, this region was still covered by mile-thick ice caps. As the climate warmed, the ice caps melted and the glaciers receded, leaving a raw and naked land strewn with glacial till and debris, seamed with the jumbled rocks of terminal moraines and meandering sandy eskers, the accumulated sediment of long-ago sub-glacial streams. ❖ Pioneering  plants—tough lichens and mosses, low birches and creeping willows—covered the naked earth. Slowly the somber boreal forest of hardy pines, firs, and spruces marched northward until, at the treeline, it reached the limit of possible growth and ceded sovereignty to the treeless tundra, a land as vast and lonely as the sea. ❖ Life hangs in balance between growth and destruction for the spruces at the treeline. Most are marked by the never-ending struggle to survive. Snow protects the nascent trees in winter. But as the trees grow and poke above the snow, they are exposed to the full fury of winter winds which carry needle-sharp spicules of snow and ice that blast the buds and shear the delicate sprouts of summer. Only on the leeward side can branches survive on the upper part of the trunk, receiving meager but vital protection from the trunk itself, so that from afar the spruces look like ragged, wind-torn weathervanes.  "Flagged trees," botanists call them, and to the Cree Indians this is "The Land of the Little Sticks." ❖ In this region of many lakes and stunted trees south of the present town of Churchill is the southernmost important denning area of female polar bears. Their winter presence here has been observed for centuries. In the 1770s, the famous Hudson's Bay Company trader and explorer Samuel Hearne wrote that although most bears go out onto the ice of Hudson Bay to hunt seals, "the females that are pregnant seek shelter at the skirts of the woods, and dig themselves dens into the deepest drifts of snow they can find, where they remain in a state of inactivity, and without food, from the latter end of December or January, till the latter end of March; at which time they leave their dens and bend their course towards the sea with their cubs; which, in general, are two in number." The exact location of this denning area was discovered by the biologist Charles Jonkel in the winter of 1969-1970. ❖ This same biologist, during a meeting in Ottawa in the early 1960s, suggested I should come along as an unpaid assistant on his first major study of polar bears. We spent the summer on Southampton and Coats Islands in northern Hudson Bay and the fall on the southwest coast of Hudson Bay, trapping and tagging polar bears. ❖ I already knew polar bears, but only as prey. I lived for several years with the Inuit. These people deeply respect polar bears, and long ago worshipped them. They also hunt polar bears, eat their fat and meat, and dress in their furs or sell the pelts. One year, I joined two Inuit brothers from Grise Fjord on Ellesmere Island {the northernmost settlement in Canada} and their eldest sons on the last of the great Inuit polar bear hunts; a two-month, twelve-hundred-mile trip by dog team, living entirely off the land. ❖ Working with Jonkel was different; we did not kill bears. We captured, marked, and weighed them. This was the beginning of intensive and systematic polar bear research in Canada. That summer with the polar bears was the beginning of a lifelong passion. ❖ Polar bears are highly individualistic animals. When one first observes or studies polar bears, they are majestic but anonymous, powerful creatures superbly adapted to their icy realm. "They are the unrivaled master-existences in this icebound solitude," wrote the famous naturalist John Muir after he saw polar bears on the ice off Alaska in 1899. ❖ Polar bears are not territorial animals. They roam far in search of prey, yet years of study have shown that their wanderings are not nearly as haphazard as was once assumed. Most bears of a region stay within that region {it may be larger than England}, know it, follow predictable hunting paths and patterns through the seasons which are determined by the presence or absence of sea ice. At Cape Churchill, for instance, many of the bears that gather there each fall are "regulars," familiar bears that return to the cape year after year at a certain time, in some cases for more than twenty years. It is simply part of their seasonal cycle of travel. ❖ Most female polar bears use the same denning areas every two or three years to bear their tiny cubs in mid-winter. It usually is the denning area where, years earlier, they were born. Cubs stay with their powerful, protective mother for several years and learn from her the hunting skills that assure their future survival. Polar bears live in a world of smells. Each breeze carries with it myriad messages that guide the bear and determine its actions. ❖ Slowly, as one learns more and more about polar bears, one becomes familiar with certain individuals and can anticipate their behavior, it becomes a magic voyage into the realm of another creature, an animal with a complex hierarchical social structure living in one of the harshest climatic regions on earth.

Under the rising sun, two polar bears, a female and her cub, stand on the frozen sea ice, twenty miles north of Cape Churchill. The female mated two years before in April, when she was four years old, and her cub was born in a snow den fifty miles south of the cape. For the first year the cub was obedient, following his mother over the sea ice, waiting patiently as she hunted seals. Now, at 200 pounds, the cub is nearly as large as his mother, though not as heavy. In that late-teen age between dependence and independence, he

ignores her vocalized warning calls, yet continues to rely on her for food and protection. ❖
Now, in mid-March, after a lengthy hunt and ample feast of seal blubber and meat, the
two bears stretch out in the lee of a pressure-ridge and sleep in the warming sun. Abruptly,
the female rises without making a sound. She climbs the ice ridge, looks back once more
upon her sleeping cub, and walks fast and purposefully out of his life. The cub awakens,
warm, well-fed, and content. He yawns, stretches languorously, and calls his mother.
There is no answer. He searches for her, calls and whines, picks up her track and follows
it, but slowly, as if aware that the bond has been broken. After a while he veers off, walking alone across the vastness of the ice.

In mid-April the female comes into estrus. She urinates frequently, the enticing scent spreads far, and
soon an eager throng of suitors follows her. They fight fiercely among themselves until a great 900-pound
male arrives, quickly defeats all rivals and drives them off. She and the great male travel together for eight
days and mate frequently. Suddenly her odor and her attitude change. She repels his advances; he quickly loses interest and walks away in search of another receptive female. ❖ Within her womb, two fertilized
ova divide, and divide again and again on the path to new life. Then suddenly, they cease to develop,
remaining dormant in their mother's womb. During the three months between April and June, the female
achieves one of nature's most astounding feats: she accumulates sufficient fat to fuel an eight-month fast,
during which time she will give birth and raise two cubs—all three animals living entirely off her fat
reserves. ❖ Since April, the female has been "a little bit pregnant." Her two fertilized ova developed to
slightly more than pinhead size, then suddenly ceased to grow, motes of life in suspended animation. In
September, subtle hormonal changes reactivate their growth. Implantation, so long delayed, takes place,
bringing with it normal embryonic development.

The female's seemingly aimless northward rambles, between long rests, have brought her
to the latitude where she was born and where, three years ago, she gave birth to her first
cub. Now, in early December, she purposefully walks from the coast inland. Once she has
reached the ancestral denning area among the gnarled and ragged spruces, she begins a
long, deliberate, exacting search for an ideal snow slope. ❖ Inuit do the same thing before
building an igloo. Some anthropologists suspect they may have learned the technique by
watching polar bears. The Inuit test the snow with a subgut, a long thin probe of caribou

antler with an ovoid ferrule at one end and a handle at the other, trying to find OQAALUG-SAIT, hard-packed, fine-grained snow deposited by a single storm. This is the ideal raw material from which to cut the large igloo building blocks. ❖ The female bear is just as fussy. She scrapes into a drift and quickly abandons it. The snow is not firm enough. Another drift is too thin. After hours of trying and testing, she finds exactly what she wants; a bowl-shaped slope filled with hard-packed snow. ❖ Finally satisfied, she digs with speed and assurance. Her massive sharp-clawed paws sweep away the top layer of soft snow, then dig a narrow entrance up into the slope that, like the upward-sloping entrance to an igloo, acts as a cold trap. Since warm air is lighter than cold air, none of it will escape downward from the den. ❖ At first loose snow and chunks of snow rush and roll down the slope. As she proceeds upward, the dug-out snow is packed into the tunnel behind her and plugs the entrance. At the upper end the female excavates an oval chamber, approximately eight feet long, six feet wide and only five feet high. The walls of hard, compacted snow are patterned by the deep score marks of her claws. ❖ Outside, wind and snow soon efface all traces of the den. Inside it is cozy. The many air cells in the snow make it an excellent insulator. The temperature inside the den can be forty degrees Fahrenheit warmer than the temperature outside. The female scrapes a small air vent into the roof of the den to let stale air escape, then rubs and rolls on the den floor until she is comfortable. Immured now for many months, she begins to doze. Outside, the short winter day ends. The evening wind soughs through the scraggly spruces. Small flocks of busy boreal chickadees feed and whisper for a while in the snow-covered branches and then begins the icy stillness of the northern night. ❖ In the darkness of her den, shielded from the hostile upper earth, the female bear sleeps on for days and weeks, lass and lethargic. Her body motor idles softly—her body temperature several degrees lower than normal, her heart rate slower than normal, expending a minimum of energy. She does not eat nor does she drink since metabolized fat provides her both energy and water. ❖ Her two cubs, a male and female, are born in the first days of January. They seem pathetically ill-prepared to leave the cozy 102 degrees Fahrenheit warmth of their mother's womb for life in a snow den in the midst of an arctic winter. Since only four months have passed since implantation and the growth of the two fetuses began, the newborn cubs are tiny. The male weighs one-and-a-half pounds, the female one-quarter pound less. These baby bears that will someday grow to be the largest land carnivores on earth—top weight for male polar bears is more than fifteen

hundred pounds—start life the size of rats. ❖ They are blind and deaf, their pink bodies covered with sparse, whitish, fuzzy wool, except for their rust-red noses and the pink pads of their tiny paws. The cubs may be tiny and poorly developed but instinct tells them exactly what to do. Clinging with sharp, sickle-shaped claws to the fur of their mother, the cubs climb toward her chest and begin to suckle her fat-rich milk. Polar bear milk contains thirty-one percent butterfat and twelve percent protein—compared to four percent butter-fat in cow's milk—and is surpassed in nutritional value only by the milk of seals and whales. ❖ The female does not lie prone in the den. Most of the time she reclines, in the position of an ailing Victorian dowager propped up in bed to receive visitors for tea. The cubs cuddle into her deep-pile fur. When they are cold, they whimper. The mother cradles them with her huge paws and breathes over them to keep them warm. While the cubs live encapsulated in the security of their den and the embrace of their mighty mother, the winter sky above is aflame with the spectral dance of the aurora borealis, for the denning area is precisely in the path of the northern auroral zone.

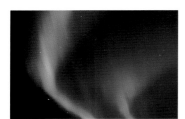

The Cree Indians believe, recorded Samuel Hearne in 1772, that the northern lights were "the spirits of their departed friends dancing in the clouds; and when [the light] is remarkably bright...they say, their deceased friends are very merry." On clear moonless nights, great pale green curtains soar into heaven. They flare and flow in eerie splendor against the velvet black of night, changing to deep violet and back to pale green again. ❖ Only females with newborn cubs den all winter. All other polar bears den occasionally to avoid vicious arctic storms with wind-whipping, blinding snow and searing cold. Polar bears, magnificently protected by fur and fat, are not likely to die in the wildest winter storm. But even for the bears, walking in such cruel weather is unpleasant and a waste of energy, so they avoid it. At the onset of a storm, a polar bear digs a shallow snow pit, curls up in it, and is quickly covered by a blanket of drifting snow. In this day-bed the bear sleeps through the storm in cozy comfort.

Far to the north of the mother bear's den, a fierce winter gale screams through Lancaster Sound in Canada's high Arctic. As the storm abates, a wind-smoothed drift stirs and cracks, and like a mound of snow coming to life, a great polar bear rises from his pit. He shakes loose snow out of his fur, and because his skin itches, rolls and rubs luxuriously on the hard-packed, wind-fluted snow. One more shake and he is instantly dry, for his dense,

oily wool and shaggy coat of guard hairs do not retain snow and moisture. ❖ In former days, the Inuit used this property of polar bear fur to ice the runners of their sleds. A piece of fur was dipped in warm water and slipped smoothly over the sled runners, coating them with a film of ice, thus reducing friction and making it easier for the huskies to haul the sled and its load. With a flick of his hand, the Inuk driver could shake the water and ice from the piece of fur, leaving it dry and supple. ❖ The bear is a male near his prime and weighs nearly one thousand pounds. He stands stolid for a while, his head and neck swaying slightly from side to side as he tests the air and allows his brain to interpret the multiple sensory messages. Finally he walks west, immense power in slow motion, thick wads of muscle rippling beneath his immaculate coat. ❖ His body is bulky; high-rumped, low-shouldered, and densely furred. The neck is long and sinuous, the head massive and triangular. His small eyes are deep brown. The nose is large, mobile, coal black and minutely pitted. The legs are short and stout, nearly columnar; the huge fur-fringed paws sharp clawed and rough in texture. His movements are slow and deliberate but that peculiar, ponderous gait is partly an illusion created by the bear's great bulk. ❖ The appearance of an aimless amble is misleading. The great male has not eaten for many days. He is ravenously hungry and alert. His sense of sight is about the same as a human's, though now, in the arctic darkness, it helps him little in the hunt. His hearing is excellent, his sense of smell acute. As our world is primarily visual, his is mostly olfactory. Minute molecular nuances borne on the wind tell him about all that lives, and moves, or simply exists in an amazingly large area. The Alaskan Inuit have an ancient saying that a polar bear can smell a whale carcass on the beach from fifty miles away. ❖ To the great bear on Lancaster Sound, one scent, above all others, is of vital interest—the smell of seal. The polar bear can sense a seal's breathing hole, covered by three feet of hard, compacted arctic snow, from more than three-quarters of a mile away. He walks, stops, tests the wind, and walks on. And every time he moves, a sinewy, cat-sized creature, a hundred yards behind him, moves too. It is a three-year-old arctic fox and the polar bear is his great provider. ❖ The fox, brindled brown in the summer, is now in silky, snow-white winter fur. His gorgeous coat, perhaps the warmest in the world, provides such perfect insulation for his seven-pound body that, when he is sleeping on a windswept ridge at minus-forty degrees, he is as warm as a human on a tropical beach. Cold is not a problem for foxes, but food is. Winter is a hungry season. This fox picked up the trail of the great male polar bear in late November

and has been with him ever since, living on leftovers. Lately, because of the storm, there has been no food for either of them. He follows with that insouciance the swift offer up to irritate the slow, mixed with some deference and justifiable caution. ❖ Twice the dozing bear has risen soundlessly and walked to his sleeping companion. Yet each time, as the bear tenses for a deadly pounce, the fox—who is a very light sleeper for just this reason—wakes up and shoots away. In this way the bear shows that the fox irks him, and that he never forgets the fox is there. ❖ The fox, on the other hand, has a certain proprietary feeling for the bear. In late December, another younger fox tries to share his fortune; that fox is promptly attacked. Backs arched, tails stiffly raised like flags of war, the two foxes growl and snap. After a while, the younger fox leaves to look for a bear of his own. ❖ Now both fox and bear are hungry. Dark shapes, one huge and one tiny, move through the diaphanous blue of the arctic night, guided by the bear's sense of smell. At last he stops. Invisible beneath the snow is an aglu, the breathing hole of a ringed seal. The bear knows through experience and smell that this one has been recently and repeatedly used. He lies down where he will wait, without making the slightest sound or movement, for hours or days.

Despite its often harsh winter weather, Lancaster Sound is, as Inuit and polar bears have known for ages, one of the richest sea-mammal regions in the entire north, an arctic Eden discovered by Commander William Parry of Britain's Royal Navy in the summer of 1819. He was amazed and delighted for he had found "the headquarters of the whales." Giant bowhead whales lolled lazily on the dark sea—on July 30, Parry and his crew counted eighty-nine. "Sea horses [walruses] lay upon the ice floes huddled together like pigs...stupidly tame." Polar bears ambled nonchalantly across the ice. White whales were "swimming about the ship in great numbers [making] a shrill ringing sound, not unlike that of musical glasses badly played." Ivory-tusked narwhals, called "sea-unicorns" by sailors, surged through the sea. And not mentioned by Parry, but of great importance to the chain of life in the Arctic, is the ringed seal. These seals, along with the larger, less-common bearded seals, are the main prey of Inuit and polar bears. ❖ Lancaster Sound is still an arctic oasis, one of those magic places of the Far North where life is marvelously concentrated. True, some of the marvel and magic is gone; whalers killed the placid bowhead whales for oil and baleen. Of the ten thousand that lived in the region in Parry's time, only about a hundred are left. But large pods of white whales still swim through Lancaster Sound; it is home to most of the world's narwhals. Three million seabirds nest on cliffs lining its shores. More than a quarter million seals call it home as well; they support a population of roughly one thousand polar bears.

THE PROMISE OF LIGHT

The Polar Inuit of northwest Greenland, the northernmost people on earth, call February SEQINNIAQ, "the month when the sun appears." At this latitude, the sun disappears in October. As it descends, the cool green horizon flushes with salmon pink, faint shafts of roseate light spread into heaven. Near noon, the sun appears, deep orange, squat, massive, and distorted, shimmering in the icy air. It hangs briefly on the edge of the world, its last rays flickering across the frozen land. Then it sinks away, and darkness lies upon the land. ❖ The sun rises again in February, a sullen, orange-red disk that floods the arctic world with light. The Inuit shout the ancient greeting: SAINANG SUNAI SEQINEQ! Praised be the sun! ❖ Yet for all its promise of light and life, February is the month the Inuit fear most. Throughout much of the arctic it is the month of storms that makes hunting difficult or impossible. In February, provisions laid up for winter dwindle rapidly.

The female polar bear in her den cares nothing for the winter storms that rage outside. In her snow lair, among the wind-torn spruces west of Hudson Bay, she and her cubs are cozy and secure. But it is now seven months since she has eaten much of anything. Her ever-hungry, rapidly growing cubs consume her blubber layer via fat-rich milk. ❖ The cubs are now cat-sized, but chubbier, with round furry paws, and coats of dense, soft, fluffy wool covered by coarser guard hairs. The male is noticeably larger and more assertive than his sister. When the cubs are twenty-six days old, they begin to hear; at thirty-three days their eyes open. Whenever they are hungry, the cubs mewl and nudge their mother; she leans slightly forward and they nurse urgently, rapidly, changing frequently from one of the four pectoral nipples to another, pushing her great chest with their little paws. The female reclines with her eyes closed. From time to time she licks her cubs, partly in deep affection, partly to keep them clean. She also keeps the den clean. When its floor becomes soiled with the cubs' urine and feces, she covers it with a layer of fresh snow scraped from the ceiling and walls of the den. ❖ At forty-five days old, the cubs begin to explore their small domain in crepuscular light that, on brilliantly sunny days, faintly brightens the dome of their den. They traipse and romp and grapple and sometimes they squeal. Their mother is sleepy. She reclines against the den wall and dozes, expending as little energy as possible. But should any danger threaten, she would instantly awaken. ❖ The Canadian scientist Richard

Harington once opened the roof of a den on Southampton Island in Hudson Bay—"A glistening black eye and twitching muzzle were instantly applied to the aperture by the mother bear. While she paced the den floor beneath us, uttering peevish grunts, we were just able to discern her two young cubs huddled against the far wall of their snow house."

Polar bears are opportunistic feeders. Given the chance, they will eat anything, from tiny lemmings to large whales and rarely, humans. They can consume vast quantities of food. A large polar bear, if very hungry, will eat up to one hundred-fifty pounds of blubber at one meal. In one sitting, a polar bear ate one thousand eider duck eggs {in volume the equivalent to 2,000 hen's eggs}, the winter store of one of my Inuit friends. While polar bears have definite food preferences, they will eat with equal zest putrid whale carrion and discarded motor oil. These are incidental meals. Seals are their staple food, their staff of life. ❖ The polar bear's realm is immense; five million square miles of circumpolar land and frozen sea. Its distribution overlaps, on sea ice, roughly that of the seven to eight million ringed seals that inhabit the arctic seas. Where ringed seals are common, as in Hudson Bay {with an estimated population of 500,000} or in Lancaster Sound, polar bears are usually common. Where ringed seals are rare or absent, polar bears tend to be rare or absent. The lives of the two animals are closely linked. Just as it is every polar bear's main aim in life to catch, kill, and eat ringed seals, every ringed seal's major preoccupation in life is not to be caught and eaten by polar bears. ❖ Arctic land mammals must be able to endure winter temperatures that can drop to minus-sixty Fahrenheit; combined with high winds this would kill a naked human in about seven minutes. Sea mammals seem to have it easier because the temperature of the Arctic Ocean never falls below twenty-eight degrees. However, heat conduction in water is about twenty-five times greater than in air; it can suck the vital warmth quickly from a living animal. Walruses, seals, and whales survive the cold by being sheathed in blubber, two to three inches thick on a seal and nearly two feet thick on a bowhead whale. They are like animated thermos bottles; a body core kept warm by a non-conductive shell of insulating blubber. Rich in calories and energy, blubber is the polar bear's preferred and principal food. ❖ A large male ringed seal is about five feet long and weighs around 150 pounds. Females are slightly smaller. In fall, as ice begins to cover the arctic seas, bays and inlets, each ringed seal cuts as many as ten to fifteen breathing holes in the ice with the long sharp claws of its foreflippers. They keep these cone-shaped holes open through ice, which in midwinter may be six feet thick, as vital vents to the air above. In the murky world beneath the ice, the seal hunts arctic cod or crustaceans. After diving for five to fifteen minutes, the seal surfaces in one of the holes, breathes deeply for ten to thirty seconds to reoxygenate his body, and then dives again. ❖ An Inuk finds a seal's breathing hole, an aglu, with the help of trained

dogs. He inserts an idlak, a long sliver of wood or bone, through the overlying snow into the breathing hole, a colored tassel or feather attached to its top. He spreads a piece of thick caribou winter fur upon the snow to muffle even the slightest noise from his feet. Sound carries far in water. A seal can hear the crunch-crunch-crunch of a man walking on hard arctic snow from more than a thousand feet away, and the tiniest noise will warn it of danger. ❖ The hunter bends over, like a three-quarter-closed jackknife and stands in this position, immobile. Since every ringed seal has many breathing holes, it may be hours, or even days, before the seal surfaces in the breathing hole where the hunter waits. I have seen Inuit stand like this, still as statues, in bitter cold and cutting wind, for more than twenty hours, their entire beings concentrated upon that tiny tassel. When the seal finally surfaces it touches the idlak, the tassel moves, and in one smooth, powerful motion the Inuk drives his harpoon through the snow into the seal. ❖ It seems likely that ages ago, Inuit learned the essence of aglu hunting by observing polar bears. Inuit boys, at first, are rarely successful at this hunt. They pick the wrong aglu, or they move too much and thereby warn the seal, or impatient, they run from aglu to aglu, hoping for luck and a quick kill. Young polar bears make the same mistakes. They simply lack the patience required for this hunt. They wait for a while at an aglu, give up and roam the ice, hoping to find the remains of seals left by older bears. Often, adolescent bears, recently abandoned by their mothers, eat little more than the remains left by other bears. ❖ Adult bears, like the great male on Lancaster Sound, excel at aglu hunting. It suits him for it promises the greatest caloric reward for the least exertion and expenditure of energy. All he has to do is lie and wait; quite pleasant occupations for a polar bear. The day is cold but the bear is warm, protected by a thick layer of fat and a magnificent, double-layered fur with special insulating properties. ❖ John V. E. Hansen, who worked at U.S. Army laboratories designing protective clothing for U.S. soldiers, examined the polar bear's white hair. Using a scanning electron microscope he discovered that each strand is both transparent and hollow so that it can transmit solar energy, including that in the ultraviolet range, to the animal's coal-black skin, where it is absorbed as heat.

The great male waits, warm, relaxed, slightly hunched, alert and infinitely patient. Hours pass. He never moves. Suddenly there is a change in smell, a rush of air as the seal surfaces beneath the snow and the faint, sometimes snorting or bubbling sound of its inhalation. The bear tenses and with one blow of enormous power, breaks the snow cover and pins the seal against the aglu's side. Grabbing it nearly simultaneously with his teeth, he crushes the thin-boned skull and yanks the carcass out of the constricted hole with a force great enough to break most of its elastic ribs. The bear bites the seal repeatedly on the head and neck, then hauls it a few feet away from the aglu and begins to eat. ❖ Even though this is his first meal in many days, the bear eats methodically. He holds the carcass down with both sharp-clawed paws, bites into it, rips out a piece of skin and fat, chews, and swallows it. He licks up blood and eats some of the entrails. From time to time he pauses to lick his bloodied paws. ❖ The pace of this feasting is frustrating for the hungry fox. He sits near-by and stares at the feeding bear with light amber, slanted eyes, dashes in for just one bite, but pirouettes away as the great bear growls and threatens. ❖ The bear eats for more than an hour: all of the skin and blubber, most of the entrails and the blood, including some of the blood-soaked snow, and since he is very hungry, much of the meat. Full, the bear moves aside and cleans himself with utmost care. He rubs and rolls in the snow and licks his muzzle, chest, and paws until not even the slightest stain mars his silver-glistening fur. Matted, dirty fur, no doubt, loses some of its effectiveness as a solar heat convector. ❖ The  bear's prolonged clean-up has finally given the fox his chance. He rushes to the remains of the seal and rips, chews, and gulps with frantic urgency, keeping at all times a careful eye on the bear. His caution is justified, for the bear begrudges the fox his food. Driven by what psychologists call futterneid {food envy} the bear suddenly rushes at the fox and chases him away from the seal. He eats a bit more meat and then, as if in spite, lies down close to his kill and dozes, threatening and growling each time the famished fox comes close.

A FICKLE SEASON

March, in most of the Arctic, is still winter. Its cold and vicissitudes bothered nineteenth-century explorers so much that in their massive tomes they complained at length about the "roaring and hissing" of March storms and "the oppressive stillness and solitude" of quiet days. ❖ True, March is fickle, and can be cruel, but often it is sublime: the month of promise, of light and life, of resurrection after midwinter darkness and dormancy. The air is cold and clear, the sky a robin's-egg blue, turning to cool green near the horizon. Snow and ice are brilliantly aglitter. The sun, so weak and wan on winter days, has strength and warmth. Late in the evening the sun's last rays slant across land and ice, flecking the snowcrests with nacre and gold. ❖ On land, beneath their protective, insulating winter blanket of snow, lemmings mate and multiply, two activities at which they excel. They are chubby rodents of the Far North, four inches long from tip of nose to tip of tiny tail, with rounded rumps, minute furry ears and feet, shiny-black button eyes, and rampant libidos. Female lemmings are alarmingly precocious and fecund. In early March, the first litters are born in their globular grass nests beneath the snow. The bee-sized babies are naked, blind, and squeaky. They suckle greedily, double their weight every four days, and are weaned at about fourteen days. Shortly thereafter, the twenty-day-old, just-weaned females mate and, after a twenty-day gestation period, produce their own litters. At about the same time their mothers, who often mate while nursing one litter, are producing their second litter of the year. ❖ In peak lemming years {usually every fourth year} the tundra can be aswarm with lemmings, hyperactive and voracious. "Fat, busy, agile mowing machines," the famous Oxford ecologist Charles Elton called them. In their millions, they can denude the tundra, but they also provide a nearly limitless feast for arctic predators. Sometimes even massive polar bears get into the act. They prance and pounce and swat the odd lemming to pulp before they eat it—a lot of effort for a meager meal. ❖ The Arctic is not lifeless in winter but its life is hidden and difficult to see. In this white and silent land, most animals are also white and usually silent. The most startling exception is the raven, the bird "with the highest mental development of all," according to the Nobel-prize winning ethologist Konrad Lorenz. The ravens are glossy blue-black all year. In winter, like

the arctic foxes, they often follow hunting polar bears, eating leftovers. The Polar Inuit know this and when, during travels, they see ravens flying purposefully over the ice, they sometimes follow them. ❖ The ravens court in late February and in March, at least a month earlier than any other arctic bird. Ravens love to fly, and they fly superbly, especially during their airborne courtship dances. High in the pale blue sky they swoop and loop and barrel roll, soaring towards heaven, then tumble earthward in intricate patterns of delight. In the stillness of the North, their ecstatic croaking seems to break the icy spell of winter. ❖ Another noisy suitor is the normally silent arctic fox. In late March the fox who followed the large male polar bear on Lancaster Sound all winter has one last seal feast, gorging himself on generous leftovers. The bear has killed many seals lately and now eats only blubber. ❖ The fox skirts the great polynya, the open water region of Lancaster Sound, crosses the ice to Somerset Island, and wanders over the rolling hills near the upper Cunningham River, until he picks up the scent of a willing vixen. For the next ten days the serenity of the Arctic is broken by the screeching and caterwauling of the pair. Finally, they set up home in an old den, dug into the sandy soil of a south-facing slope, overlooking a valley. In summer, one can see the den from far away, for in this drab, dun-colored, nutrient-poor land, it is lush-green with plants fertilized by fox scat and the bones, blood, and feathers of their prey. ❖ For polar bears, March and April are the beginning of the good life. Hunting is easier this time of the year and food is plentiful; they replenish their depleted reserves. Young, inexperienced bears who barely made it through the winter, now hunt with increasing confidence and success. Some follow large males who kill seal after seal and eat only the fat to acquire weight and power for the fights of the April mating season. ❖ In March and April, single

females begin to lay up the thick blubber reserves that will enable them to survive next season's marathon fast. For females who wintered in dens with newborn cubs, the eight-month fast is nearly ended.

In March the female in the den beneath the gnarled spruces digs a tunnel to the outside world. When she built the den in the first days of December, she was a compact vat of fat. Now she is lean and appears long-legged. She has lost nearly 400 pounds during her fast. ❖ While the mother has slimmed rapidly, her cubs have grown with amazing speed. In the two months since their birth they have expanded into densely furred, roly-poly mini-bears the size of fox terriers, but stout-legged and bulkier. The male cub weighs twenty-seven pounds, his sister twenty-three pounds and both are full of energy, all drawn from a mother who has eaten nothing for eight months. It is a physiological feat matched by no other mammal. ❖ For the cubs, the opening of their natal den is like a second birth. For a day or two they dare not leave the womb-like warmth and security of their dim den for the dazzling, alien world outside. They crawl as far as the tunnel entrance and huddle together, two snow-white little heads with rounded furry ears, black noses, and black shiny eyes that peer at the strange new world. ❖ In the vicinity of recently vacated polar bear dens one often finds large piles of dung, evidently of plant matter. This observation is the basis for a long-lived northern myth: in fall, before hibernation, the female bear stuffs her anal orifice with a massive plug of mosses and grasses to ease hunger pains and keep the den clean; once she leaves the den in spring, she excretes it all. ❖ The facts are physiologically much more fascinating. During her long fast, the female's entire digestive system has stopped working, her kidneys have ceased to function. She has not eaten or drunk in many months, nor has she urinated or defecated. ❖ Now, while the cubs hover anxiously in the den entrance, the mother walks to the base of the slope, scrapes the snow away and eats mosses, sere grasses, and lichens, together with a lot of snow, to reactivate long-dormant organs. The results are these heaps of plant-based dung. ❖ The cubs, though similar in appearance, are very different in temperament. The little female is timid and gentle; her brother is brash, more venturesome, and sometimes a bully. It is the male who first leaves the den and runs over to his mother on stubby, stumbly legs. His sister follows cautiously. ❖ At first the cubs play a little and rest a lot, usually in the den, their familiar home and haven. But they are full of life and excitement and soon they run and romp and

wrestle in the snow. On the fourth day, they discover a marvelous game. They run to the top of a snow slope, glissade down with outstretched paws, and land in piles of powdery snow. ❖ The mother watches the antics of her cubs. If they roam too far, she calls them with a low growl and they come immediately. The play gives them the strength and agility they will need for the long march to the sea. It also makes them very hungry, and they want to nurse often, rapidly draining their mother's remaining fat reserves. A storm holds them in the den for two days and then, ten days after they first emerged, they head for the sea and seals. ❖ Among the spruces at the treeline, the snow is deep and soft. The cubs try to follow in their mother's huge paw prints, but their legs are short; they sink deep into the snow and advance by exhausting jumps. It is fun at first, but soon they tire. The mother stops often to let them rest. Where the snow is very deep, the cubs crawl onto her broad back, grasp her fur with sharp-clawed paws and ride along like small jockeys. ❖ The female, as if guided by a lodestar, walks in a precise, straight line in the northeasterly direction that will take her to good seal hunting grounds on Hudson Bay ice. From time to time she stops, scoops out a shallow pit, reclines, and lets her weary little wanderers nurse. Once on the ice, the female leads her cubs to a series of pressure ridges, an area where, beneath snow drifts, female ringed seals have recently excavated birth lairs for their pups. Many polar bears hunt in this region and the female is alert and guarded. ❖ Females and females with cubs she ignores, but large males she avoids. Large males, while not at all averse to killing and eating a cub when they can do so with little or no risk, are loathe to tackle a mother, for she will fight to the death for her cubs, and in such a fight even a powerful male may get severely hurt. Long ago, the Norwegian explorer-scientist Fridtjof Nansen wrote of female polar bears and their cubs: "She shows the greatest tenderness for them, and never leaves them even in the utmost danger." ❖ The female is fortunate. In the second nunarjak {as Inuit call the birth lairs of ringed seals} that she breaks open, she kills both pup and mother. The little pup is gone in a few bites, but she eats the adult seal with methodical determination. The cubs crawl close, fascinated. They tear off snippets of soft blubber and lick up blood. For their mother, this is her first meal in eight months.

WANDERING THE SEA ICE

In the vivid imagery of their poems, Inuit call the polar bear PIHOQAHIAQ, "the ever-wandering one." It was once believed that polar bears roam at random across the immensity of the Arctic, from continent to continent, eternal nomads of the north. During the past thirty years scientists from all the northern polar bear nations have captured, marked, and recaptured thousands of polar bears. Their studies conclusively show that most polar bears belong to geographically discrete populations whose movements follow seasonal and predictable patterns. ❖ In this, as in so much else, the Inuit of former days were similar to polar bears. The explorer and scientist Graham W. Rowley, who lived at Igloolik in northern Hudson Bay fifty years ago, found that almost every Inuk knew "the country within a radius of three hundred miles or so. A comparable figure in an English village before the First World War would probably be about five miles [roughly the home range of a black bear!]—one-sixtieth the distance, or nearly one four-thousandth the area." ❖ The Inuk called Ekalun of Bathurst Inlet, with whom I lived for seven months, was about ten years old when his tribe was "discovered" by white explorers. He was one of the last Inuit to remember pre-contact times, when whites were a myth. He was familiar with a region bigger than Belgium. In this vast area, he knew the dens of wolves, the paths of caribou, the valleys with muskoxen, the outcrops where soapstone for seal oil lamps could be cut, the river valley where chunks of iron pyrite {formerly used to strike fire} could be found, the best bays with seal aglus, and the camps and names of all other Inuit in an even larger region—an immense amount of knowledge that helped make him a successful hunter in a hostile land. ❖ The polar bear has a problem not faced by other predators. The most vital part of his home range is evanescent; the sea ice where he hunts seals melts and vanishes in summer and fall and does not form again until late fall or early winter.

All March and into April the great male on Lancaster Sound hunted seals with determination and success. During the lean winter months he lost about one hundred pounds. Since then he has gained two hundred and now walks in mighty power. ❖ Polar bears are not really snow white, as is so often said. The usual color of their fur is a soft, lemon-colored wash, or the mellow yellow of ancient ivory. But in spring and early summer a few bears, perhaps bleached by the intense sun, turn glossy white. The majestic male is one of them. As he walks across the ice, his fur ripples in silvery waves with each movement of his muscled, fat-padded body. At present he is a monarch with one mission—to mate as frequently as possible. ❖ Since only about one third of all adult females come into estrus each year {the others are busy with cubs} there are, in any given area, more interested males than females. As a result, the males compete fiercely. ❖ The great male walks in a straight line with concentrated assurance. He crosses dozens of bear tracks—they do not interest him. Suddenly he veers. He has found the scent trail of an estrus female. She walks slowly, but when he catches up six other males are already following her, strung out in roughly hierarchical order. Nearest is a nine-year-old, the most serious contender, and then bears of descending weight and age, trailed, at a cautious distance, by an optimistic five-year-old. The very size of the newcomer intimidates five of the males. The nine-year-old turns and fights, but he lacks the great male's power and prowess, is bitten deeply in the neck, and as he turns to flee, is raked with razor-sharp claws across his rump. ❖ The winner travels with the female for seven days, mating frequently. When she becomes pregnant, she repels him. His second conquest is as easy. But with the third attempt, his luck runs out. Leading the strung-out pack behind an inviting female is a male of equal size and power, and he is determined to fight. ❖ The rivals circle each other, heads low, ears laid back, upper lips puffed out, staring directly at one another, the ultimate signal of provocation and aggression. They chomp loudly and moan and groan in fury; froth trickles from their muzzles. Each bear seems to become more compact, exhibiting the steely tension that precedes a lightning charge. They rush at each other, their great mouths wide open, showing deadly, dagger-like ivory-yellow canines. They bite and shake furiously, and with a sharp crack one of the great male's canines snaps off at the gums. Blood gushes from his mouth. They rise up on hind legs, spar, claw, and swat, then clinch, two furry giants in deadly embrace. They rip and wrestle, grab necks, and try to throw the opponent off balance. The other males stare from a distance. The female, as if unconcerned, lies languidly upon the snow. ❖ The great males fight ferociously for many minutes and suddenly, as if on command, the combatants part. Both, wrapped in fat and fur, are severely overheated by the exertion. They pant, gulp snow to cool their bodies, and lie spread-eagled on the ice. This peculiar position has a special function. While humans sweat and dogs pant to cool their overheated bodies, polar bears have special "hot spots" located on the thinly-furred skin areas inside their thighs. Directly beneath this skin is a densely vasculated region that brings warm blood from the cooking core to the cooling surface. Both bears are bleeding but apart from the broken tooth, neither bear is seriously hurt. ❖ The second round

begins with a roar and a rush, the huge bears rise and grapple, the great male slips and his opponent, perhaps a more experienced fighter, uses that moment to tighten his hold on the other's neck and with one vicious jerk rips the skin from neck to shoulder. This ends the fight. The victor walks off with the female. ❖ The large male drops, backs off, turns and flees. The silver-shining coat is ripped and drenched with blood. Blood oozes from his mouth. If the great male is in pain, he does not show it. He seems more preoccupied with the blood on his fur and stops often to lick himself. In the clean, clear arctic air, the wound heals quickly. Within a few days the great male is hunting seals again. But he is marked for life by a dark, distinctive, chevron-shaped scar.

Triumph Of The Arctic Spring

May in the Arctic is marvelous. There is nothing in the world as jubilant, as powerfully triumphant as an arctic spring. The tundra, for many months austere in white and brown and black, is suddenly spangled with color. Small rosettes of purple saxifrage dot the sun-warmed ridges. Fuzzy, carmine-tipped catkins rise from prostrate dwarf willows. Heliotropic arctic poppies on slender stems turn their golden blooms toward the sun. ❖ It rains. The air, pure but odorless in winter, is now rich with the smell of moist earth, of life. Caribou come from the south to their summer pastures in the north, an urgent brown-gray migration. They trot across the sodden land in the blue-gray El Greco light, following dark, earthy trails worn deep into the tundra soil by endless caribou herds of ages past. ❖ Birds arrive and fill the tundra with jubilation. Ruddy turnstones in striking black and white flit from rock to rock, establishing territories. Elegant horned larks spiral toward the sky until they are but specks in the blue, then drift gently downward on set wings, singing a lilting song. ❖ Falcons return to ancient eyries used, if undisturbed, by generations of these magnificent hunters that can swoop upon their prey like bolts from heaven at 180 miles per hour. Old eyries are often easy to spot; the rock near them is spangled with the bright-orange nitrophilous jewel lichen, CALOPLACA ELEGANS, which the Polar Inuit of northwest Greenland call, less elegantly, SUNAIN ANAK, "the sun's excrement." ❖ Even on cool days, furry bumblebees buzz from bloom to bloom. This seems a physical impossibility. The wing muscles of insects do not function at temperatures below fifty degrees Fahrenheit. Yet arctic bumblebees fly noisily at temperatures far below that, when they ought to be torpid. The American scientist Bernd Heinrich unraveled this mystery in a fascinating study. Like an airplane revving up before flight, a chilly bumblebee begins to shiver so violently it raises its body temperature to ninety-five degrees Fahrenheit, sixty degrees higher than the air temperature. Then off it flies to collect high-calorie nectar, the fuel for this immense expense of energy. ❖ For bumblebee or polar bear,

for Inuk or bearded seal, as for all life everywhere on earth, the equation is essentially the same: to survive, there has to be a balance between energy acquired and energy expended. The problem in the Arctic is that short periods of plenty are followed by long periods of dearth. To equalize this, the Inuit cache surplus food while the hunting is good and polar bears gorge on seal blubber, storing it as fat on their bodies. ❖ For Inuit and polar bears, March, April, May, June, and—in the high Arctic—July, are the fat months when bearded and ringed seals are plentiful and young seals are plump and naïve. The Inuit with their boats, kayaks and umiaks, extend the harvest time into the open water season: August, September, and sometimes early October. But for the bears, once the sea ice melts, the season of plenty ends. ❖ In spring, female ringed seals cut breathing holes into ice beneath thick snowdrifts, excavate nunarjaks, and give birth to tiny ten-pound pups, wrapped in snow-white, densely curled lanugo. Fed frequently on fat-rich milk for nearly two months, the pups expand rapidly. At the age of two weeks, they molt their natal wool. Now their fur is similar to that of adult ringed seals; short and stiff, dark gray patterned with silvery-gray rosettes. At this point they are called "silver jars." At weaning time they look like bulbous butterballs, weigh forty to fifty pounds; seventy percent of their total weight is fat.

Since she reached the sea ice of Hudson Bay in late March, the female from the den beneath the spruces and her little cubs have wandered along pressure ridges on Hudson Bay, forty to fifty miles from shore where, under thick, compacted snowdrifts in the lee of upturned ice slabs, the female bear has the best chance of finding nunarjaks, the seal's birthing chamber. ❖ She meanders, guided by smell. Most of the time, like little shadows, her cubs meander behind her. The little male, however, loves to explore; he leads his more timid sister astray and the two gambol off, pounce into soft snow among the ice blocks, slide down polished slabs of ice, until their mother calls and they obediently trot back to her. ❖ When the female finds a nunarjak she uses one of two methods to get at the contents. If she suspects, by smell, that only the seal pup is at home, she digs rapidly into the drift, her sharp-clawed paws tearing out great chunks of hard snow. She excavates the pup and eats it, a small snack for so much effort. ❖ Her other method is much more dramatic. If she senses from a distance that the nunarjak is occupied by both female seal and pup, she races toward the snowdrift from forty to fifty feet away, rears high and slams her stiff, columnar front legs like pile drivers into the snow, ideally just above the breathing hole. Thus, she collapses the nunarjak and traps the adult seal and pup within, both easy victims

and a rewarding meal. ❖ Occasionally she uses a third method, a carefully thought-out stratagem. Cautiously, she tunnels into an unoccupied nunarjak directly above the breathing hole, then plugs the hole with her massive body, her head in the lair just above the water of the breathing hole, her hind end outside. She hangs there, head down, deadly and silent. ❖ The female seal is a wary creature. She will not return to a brightly-lit, broken-into lair. But if all is dark and silent and seems safe, she may surface in the breathing hole. In that instant the bear grabs her from above and hauls her out. ❖ For the female bear on the ice, nunarjak hunts are rewarding but not easy. Many lairs have already been raided by other bears. She is also an exemplary mother, totally devoted to the safety and care of her cubs, and she will skirt promising areas if she sees a large male bear or picks up his scent. Twice when she had succeeded in killing adult seals, male bears picked up her scent and that of her prey and came in a hurry. The female, huffing and hissing furiously, called her cubs and left rather than risk a battle with the male pirate who, if she was killed or severely injured in a fight, would kill and eat her cubs. ❖ Her cubs, at first, are fascinated by the seals she kills. Soon they begin to share her meals. The mother shares willingly with only a twinge of futterneid. Since she nurses the cubs frequently—and will keep nursing them for more than a year and often far into their second year—it is she who needs the food most. ❖ One day, while she tears gobs of fat and skin off a seal, a ten-pound slab of skin and fat comes loose. The male cub grabs it and hauls it away. Although his teeth and claws are needle-sharp, he does not yet know how to pin down a chunk of food and tear off bite-sized pieces. He chews at his slippery prize. It slides and he only gets little bits. When the mother is finished with her meal, most of the little male's trophy is still intact. ❖ The mother walks over, the male cub growls possessively. She lies down and inches slowly across the snow, and when she is close enough, her great paw glides softly over the snow, one sharp claw hooks into junior's chunk of food and, ever so gently, she pulls it away from him. Suddenly it is no longer his but hers; she tears it up and eats it. ❖ After the meal, mother and cubs roll and rub in the snow to clean themselves. The mother licks the cubs but they have already learned to lick themselves and to lick each other. They walk to the lee of a ridge, the mother digs a shallow pit and reclines. Her cubs nurse and, filled with milk and warmth, snuggle close to her and purr.

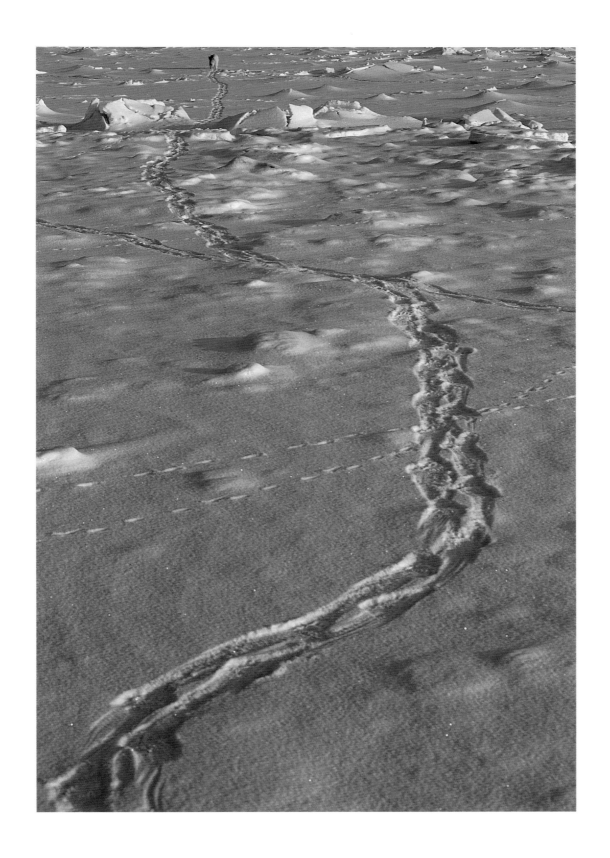

MELTING ICE

In May, the whiteness of snow and ice reflects more than ninety percent of the sun's incident energy. By June the land is rapidly becoming bare. Snow simply vanishes into the dry, sun-warmed arctic air. Meltwater murmurs down to tundra lakes and rivers in a shimmering lacework of brooks and rills. For a long time the sea ice, white and reflective, seems immune to change. ❖ In June, ice near the shore begins to melt and pools of sable water skirt the capes. Sand, gravel, and pebbles, hurled by winter storms from land far out onto the sea ice, warm up in the sun and sink tiny pits into the ice. ❖ The ice, so firm and stationary in winter, now begins to shift, ever so slightly at first, with winds and currents. Fissures and rifts, called leads, rend and seam the perfect whiteness. ❖ Polynyas, those strange arctic oases where water never freezes no matter how cold it gets, grow larger. In winter, they range in size from a circular hole in the ice of Cambridge Fjord near Baffin Island, only 250 feet in diameter, to the "North Water," as nineteenth-century whalers called it, in northernmost Baffin Bay, larger than Lake Superior. Created by a

combination of currents, winds, and upwelling water, polynyas are prodigiously rich in marine life. Inuit and polar bears patrol their rims. The Polar Inuit of northwest Greenland call the North Water polynya IMAQSSUAQ, "the great water." ❖ On spring nights, the floe edge is a fantasy-land of shimmering, wave-and-wind sculptured ice mirrored in a lambent sea. The ice glows in the soft opalescence of morning, in delicate lilac, rose, and cool green. Bone-white icicles hang in grottoes of the deepest blue. ❖ In June, meltwater floods large areas of sea ice and beneath that smooth sheen lies eroded, needle-sharp ice that is hard on the water-softened paws of polar bears and sled dogs. Bears make extensive detours to avoid the water-covered ice. ❖ Dogs are an integral part of an Inuit hunt. Traditional Inuit make bag-like sealskin booties for their dogs and tie them loosely around their legs so as to not cut off circulation. The dogs detest the booties. When an eleven-dog team is trying to rid itself of forty-four booties, travel is extremely slow. On Inuit hunting trips it was usually my duty to collect sled dog boots, then race, sweating and panting, to catch up with the sled. ❖ In June the gulls and sea ducks arrive. Common eiders woo on dark lagoons, the male striking white above, jet-black below, with a rakish black cap, partially parted with a white strip, faintly tinted with chartreuse. "A-ooo, a-ooo, a-ooo" croon the males and display for their ruddy-brown ducks. The males throw their heads back, puff out peach-colored chests, rise slightly in the water and then abruptly tilt forward. ❖ While the massive eiders fill the spring night with their mellow woodwind crooning, slender oldsquaws gather in gabby flocks in leads to chatter and natter and flirt and fight. Oldsquaws in pursuit of a mate are marvelously mad. Long-tailed males grapple and dunk each other, then rise in dizzying pursuit of a chosen female. Both zigzag in wild flight, wailing, screaming, yodeling, across ice

and land, rise high into the sky, zoom down and crash-land upon the water as if they had flunked all flying tests. ❖ Along the lead, the clear, greenish water is aswarm with life. Clouds of copepods dart about like animated rice grains. Brownish, scarlet-rimmed jellyfish pulse through the water, their diaphanous mantles expanding and contracting. Small, black-winged pelagic snails waft along with measured beat: TULUGARSSAQ, "the ones that look like ravens," the Polar Inuit call them. ❖ Mineral-rich water layers well up from the deep. Phytoplankton, sea plants so tiny that twelve million can live in a gallon of water, thrive on the minerals and also convert the sun's distant energy into living tissue. They are the base of the mighty pyramid of sea life. A bowhead whale scoops from the sea each day nearly two tons of planktonic animals, which in turn obtained that day through the sea's chain of life, the food energy of five trillion sea plants. And at the apex of that chain of life are the master sea mammal predators of the North, Inuit and polar bears. ❖ In June, ringed seals haul out onto the ice beside their enlarged breathing holes, along leads, or at the floe edge, the limit of landfast ice. In favorite regions the seals may speckle the ice as far as the eye can see—"floe rats," the whalers called them. ❖ The seals are jittery. They sleep a minute or less, wake up, raise their heads, and look carefully around to make certain no enemy is near. Satisfied that all is safe, they slump down for another short sleep. They lie at the very edge of the water-slippery ice. The instant they sense danger, they move slightly and slide smoothly into the saving sea. ❖ For the utoq hunt of basking seals, Inuit of the eastern Arctic use portable hunting screens, now of canvas, formerly of pure-white, sun-bleached sealskin. Hidden behind his shield the hunter stalks the seal, advancing with short, quick, silent steps while the seal sleeps, crouching, invisible, behind the white screen when the seal wakes up. ❖ The central Inuit use a method of utoq hunting, known from Alaska to Greenland, based on an intimate knowledge of seal behavior—they approach the seal pretending to be a seal. The hunter, prone upon the ice, times his advance to the sleep-wake rhythm of the seal. When the seal sleeps, he cautiously slithers forward. When the seal awakes, the man scratches, as with a flipper, twists, and then slumps down, apparently in sleep, so that the astigmatic seal regards him as a harmless fellow. To successfully impersonate a seal, an Inuk friend once told me, "You have to think just like a seal." This hunt requires great skill and experience. As long as the ice is dry, the hunt is tolerable. But when the ice is flooded and the hunter's clothes are soaked with icy meltwater, the hunt becomes a terrible test of endurance and fortitude.

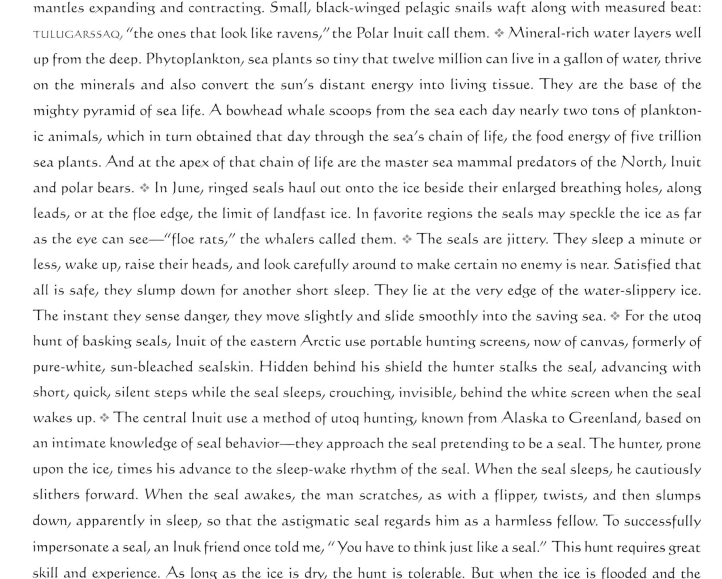

For the female and her cubs on Hudson Bay, utoq hunting brings a major change. Until now they were inseparable. But while the female stalks a seal, she must hide her cubs so they will not scare the prey. ❖ She spots a likely seal in the distance, stands up for a better look, tests the air to be certain no large male is nearby, then parks the cubs behind a slab of upright ice. She "talks" to her cubs frequently, mainly in low grunts and growls. One growl means "Stay put!" The cubs lie down obediently and the female walks until the seal is directly upwind from her, beginning her patient stalk. Like an Inuk, she times her movements to the seal's rhythm, sliding soundlessly across the ice while the seal sleeps; she freezes into immobility the instant the seal moves. The seal makes his survey, seeing only an indistinct yellowish lump upon the ice. Satisfied that all is safe, the seal goes back to sleep. ❖ When the mother bear is within seventy yards of the seal, too far for the final, fatal rush, the male cub, tired of waiting, leaves the hiding place and comes prancing and splashing across the ice. The seal wakes instantly and slides into the water. The mother walks back, cuffs the cub, and growls at him, a deep angry growl. It is the first time the mother has punished either cub and for a while the little male is cowed, meek and obedient. ❖ His

mother rests, walks on, spots another seal, hides the cubs with a stern growl, and starts another stalk. Her second seal is easy. It is a recently weaned silver jar, a young ringed seal—fat and foolish—the polar bear's favorite food. Cautiously she crawls toward the seal. The young seal glances casually about. At thirty yards she charges. Her sharp claws dig into the ice like crampons; she explodes with speed and power, a lethal blur of yellow across the ice. The naive young seal awakes and freezes for one startled look. A second

later the bear has pinned him down with a massive paw. She takes hold of his cranium and hauls the carcass away from the slippery ice edge. ❖ Her cubs continue to grow rapidly, about two or three inches every month. They become rounder, heavier. At the age of six months, the male weighs ninety pounds, his sister ten pounds less. At one year old, the male cub will be heavier than an adult man. Most of this energy for growth and activity comes from their mother's milk. Her hunting success is vital for all of them.

These inexperienced silver jars are the main food of inexperienced polar bears. Most apprentice bears stalk seals much like the older bears but with less patience and less success. ❖ A young male bear has a different method. He walks openly and casually from seal to seal, hoping to catch the odd deep sleeper. One day he is especially lucky. Ringed seals may lie close together near the edge of leads, but normally they lie singly beside breathing holes. Occasionally two or more seals lie near one breathing hole. This is not a good idea. The bear shambles towards two seals who dive simultaneously into the hole and get stuck. Hind flippers wiggle-waggle frantically as they try to squeeze down but it is too late. The young bear grabs one of them and yanks it out.

The female with cubs has had a lucky hunting streak. She killed several seals, ate well and now she dawdles over the partially-eaten carcass of her latest kill. A hungry male approaches, a young and skinny bear. He is cautious and deferential; the female is, at first, all fury. As he comes closer she charges; the cubs stay close behind her and peek around her big rump. ❖ The young male stands and signals "peace" with every nuance of posture: head high, mouth closed, eyes averted, lower lip thrust out. His behavior denotes submission. The female, hair on her neck and back abristle, huffs and chomps, but gradually her hostility decreases. She moves slowly toward the young bear, both are apprehensive. The cubs huddle behind her. The adults sniff, black noses nearly touching. Submissive, the young male sidles towards her kill. She follows, and, for a while, they stand on either side of the dead seal. The male cautiously tears off a piece. Appeased, she lets him feed. The cubs are fascinated. It is the first time in their lives that they have seen another bear so close.

A Summer Month

"In the Arctic," said the explorer and writer Peter Freuchen, "July is summer." In the Thule region of northwest Greenland it is only in July that the average temperature rises above the freezing point. June in the Arctic is fair but often fickle. In August, summer's brief glow fades rapidly. The plants' season of possible growth is about three months in the low Arctic and less than four weeks in the high Arctic. In early July, the tundra is spangled with flowers. A month later, the tiny petals have paled, wilted, and dropped. The leisurely progress from generation to generation, which in the south can last for months, is compressed into a scant six weeks here. The vital urgency to multiply, to grow, to complete the circle of life in summer's brief span is palpable. ❖ Some animals, of course, extend the season by breeding early. Baby lemmings born in grass nests beneath the snow in early March are already grandparents. The ravens courted early and then the female sat, unmoving, upon her eggs at temperatures so low that, had she left them for only a minute, they would have frozen solid. During the entire three-week incubation period and for about two weeks after the young hatched but needed their mother's warmth to survive, the female and her chicks lived entirely on food brought to her by a very busy mate. But now, as the land is rich with life, young ravens travel with the adults, eat often and well, and learn the tricks of raven life from their parents. ❖ Not all arctic animals are in a tearing hurry to get everything done in one brief summer. The rust-colored, fuzzy-furred arctic woolly bear caterpillar, Gynaephora groenlandica, takes a

leisurely fourteen years. It is the slowest-growing, longest-lived caterpillar on earth. It awakes in early summer, busily eats the carbohydrate-rich buds and leaves of arctic willow, and with the first chill of fall, lapses into death-like dormancy, indifferent to cold of minus-sixty degrees Fahrenheit. Cold cannot kill it, because the caterpillar produces its own antifreeze. It converts glycogen {a carbohydrate akin to starches} within its body to glycerol, an alcohol-type, highly freeze-resistant substance, reconverts it to glycogen in spring, wakes up, and goes on munching willow leaves. ❖ In July, depending on the year, latitude, and location, the sea ice usually breaks up. Eroded by meltwater from above and sea water from below, pushed by winds and tides and currents, the once-great sheets of ice are fragmented into a chaotic jumble of floes, glaring white with turquoise pools, separated by dark leads and lanes of open water. This immense jigsaw puzzle of ice pieces, shifting, changing, cracking, and heaving is in nearly constant motion. ❖ An experienced Inuk has an uncanny knowledge of ice, learned from elders and a lifetime of experience. First he waits, carefully studying the best route from floe to floe, then jumps flea-quick across small ice pieces scattered upon a stretch of open water. However, as a result of inertia, each piece supports him for a fraction of a second. ❖ For polar bears lean times are looming. Most bears on Hudson Bay drift ashore with the last ice and live on what meager fare the land provides. Further north, where ice lasts much longer, bears hunt on floes in open water. And there is one place off Hudson Bay where seals abound and ice lasts long and polar bears can live in plenty for an extra month in summer. ❖ In northwest Hudson Bay a great but narrow-necked bay cuts far inland. When the British explorer Christopher Middleton discovered it on July 12, 1742, he thought he had found that Holy Grail of arctic explorers, the entrance to the Northwest Passage. Instead he found a 150-mile long bay which he called *Wager Bay*, rich in whales and seals and polar bears. The whales are gone, exterminated by 19th century whalers. But Wager Bay is still rich in seals and it remains a favorite haunt of polar bears for, enclosed by ancient ice-polished rocks and spattered with multi-hued granite islets, the hemmed-in ice melts late. In some years the ice lasts until the end of August and polar bears from a large region congregate at Wager Bay to hunt seals. ❖ Polar bears are excellent but not overly-enthusiastic swimmers. Their fat layer and thick, oily, water-repellent fur protects them from the sapping chill of arctic water. They dog-paddle with huge, fur-fringed front paws, trailing their hind legs, occasionally using them as rudders. When caught on disintegrating ice far from land, they can swim steadily toward land for more than a hundred miles.

The great male roams the shifting ice fields, searching for prey. Bearded seals are hard to hunt but they are the bear's favorite target. If a ringed seal is a snack, a bearded seal is a feast; adults weigh about six hundred pounds. ❖ These large seals of the Arctic are dark gray, with deep-brown, doleful, beagle-like faces and droopy whiskers that curl like tendrils when dry. They are shallow-water seals and live, like walruses, on benthic food. Swimming across the sea floor like submarine vacuum cleaners, they suck up all that's edible: crabs, snails, sea slugs, shrimps, sculpins, flounders, or holothurian worms. A favorite is the whelk. Somehow they manage to suck the reluctant mollusks out of their whorled shells, for shells are never found in their stomachs. Between dives, they rest upon ice pans, doze and digest, and watch out for polar bears. ❖ The great bear ambles from floe to floe and swims across the channels that divide them. Suddenly he stops. He has smelled and spotted a bearded seal upon an ice pan three hundred yards away. The bear stands, head swaying slightly from side to side, and ponders strategy. ❖ He carefully lowers himself into the water and paddles, softly, softly, just below the surface, a ghostly shape in the dark water, along that maze of channels toward his prey. He surfaces from time to time, only his black nose and staring eyes, to breathe silently and peer cautiously, then swims on. At sixty yards, the bear surfaces for a final look, dives silently, swims to the floe at the exact spot where the seal lies, and suddenly shoots out of the water in a wild surge of power and spray. ❖ A mighty paw slams onto the seal, but the big, powerful, thick-skinned prey twists, rolls, and slides into the sea. For the rest of his life his skin is deeply scarred in parallel grooves cut by those fearsome, raking claws. Exploding in fury and frustration at the near miss, the bear pounds the ice in rage and glares at the water where his meal disappeared. ❖ A polar bear in rage is truly terrifying. Most polar bears are amiable {seals, no doubt, think otherwise}; humans are simply not on their menu. Polar bears that have attacked, killed, and eaten people were nearly always famished males, quite young or very old. A well-nourished polar bear is normally curious but not hostile. ❖ After his outburst of frustration and anger, the great male on Lancaster Sound simmers down. He shakes the water out of his fur in an aureole of sun-glittering spray, licks his paws, lies down, sleeps a while, then wanders on. A bearded seal lies on a large expanse of solid ice far from any lead. The bear again carefully surveys the scene, catalogs the breathing holes in the ice,

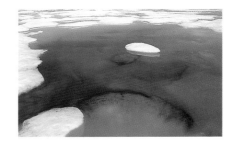

then swims beneath the ice from breathing hole to breathing hole toward the seal. Orienting himself with one final cautious glance, he swims the final leg and erupts out of the hole beside the sleeping seal. This time, the bear makes his kill and the seal dies instantly. ❖ The great bear eats, sleeps, eats more—all the blubber and much of the meat. He spends several days near his kill, leaving only the tough skin. Neatly peeled away and licked clean of the last bits of blubber, the carcass lies upon the ice. ❖ A distant chorus and a potent smell lure the bear westward. He ambles from floe to floe, swims across leads that glow in the soft light of the arctic night, leaving a faint wake of golden ripples. The sounds become louder: deep moans and groans, hoarse bellows and loud roars. A large herd of walruses rests on several floes.

Walruses like togetherness. In a sea covered with empty ice floes, they pile in chummy, madder-brown masses upon a few ice pans that nearly sink beneath their great weight, and sleep. They love to sleep; a walrus's idea of bliss is to sleep jam-packed with fellow walruses in great heaps. ❖ Physiologically it makes sense: they keep each other warm, they expend little energy, and there is might in mass. They are lethargic, somnolent beasts, until provoked by an enemy—a polar bear, Inuk, or killer whale—and then they are extremely dangerous for they attack en masse in united fury. ❖ These crowded ice floes float, conveniently, just above rich shellfish banks. To dine, the walruses merely slide off their floes, dive, and grub, head down, in the soft mud and ooze of the sea floor. Like rooting pigs, they detect food with their stiff, extremely sensitive vibrissae {their quill-like whiskers}, and slurp in mollusks with the strong suction of their puckered lips—about one thousand large clams per walrus each day. Sated, they surface, grunt and wheeze, heave their vast bulk onto a floe, and crowd together as close as possible. They squabble, groan, and jab their neighbor with sharp tusks, and finally, with deep sighs, drift off to sleep. ❖ On land or ice, polar bears occasionally kill walruses. But in water, it is the walruses who occasionally kill the nearly defenseless bear. A bull walrus comes up beneath the paddling bear, embraces him with mighty, rough-soled flippers, and drives his ivory tusks, like immense twin daggers, into the polar bear's chest.

The great bear watches the walruses from a distance, curious but cautious. Long ago, he killed an adult walrus, but it was a lucky chance. The walrus had hauled out in winter from a lead. While it slept, the ice shifted and the lead closed. The walrus could not return to the sea. Streamlined and supple in water, the mighty walrus, on land or ice, walks with a

laborious, Chaplinesque waddle. When the bear came upon the trail of the wandering walrus, the animal was weak and exhausted. It roared and hacked, but its movements were slow. The bear killed it and lived well for weeks. ❖ The night breeze eddies. The walruses catch a whiff of the bear's scent and are instantly alert. The bulls rear up and roar, their tusks flash in the slanting rays of the midnight sun and then, like a brownish avalanche, all walruses pour off their tilting floes into the safety of the sea. A few great males surface near the floe where the bear stands and bellow in fury, swiveling their protuberant, mobile, bloodshot eyes. The bear watches for a while and then lies down. This is not his game. He sleeps, the walruses swim away, regroup, and cautiously haul out on other floes. ❖ The great bear's wanderings bring him to Prince Leopold Island. Hundreds of thousands of seabirds—arctic terns, murres, fulmars, kittiwakes, guillemots, and glaucous gulls—nest on ledges, cornices or in clefts of the thousand-foot-high sheer cliffs. He circles the island. Glaucous gulls patrol all beaches and leave little for a polar bear. On the flat south spit of the island, the bear stops. A strange dark thing lies on the shingle beach. It is the inflat-able rubber boat of the ornithologists who live on top of the island and study the birds. Like all polar bears, he is cautious but curious. Anything unusual must be examined. ❖ He approaches the boat slowly from downwind, sniffs it, touches the smooth rubber with a tentative paw, and then bites into it. There is a sharp hiss of escaping air and the bear jumps back. Hissing, in polar bear society, is a signal of anger and aggression. The hissing subsides and so does one part of the boat. The bear waits and watches. Alert. Still curi-ous. He bites into another chamber—again the hiss, the startled jump backward. But he is no longer worried and by the time he is finished, the boat is in shreds. ❖ Satisfied, the bear ambles on, stopping briefly to examine the sun-bleached whale bones of long-ago Inuit dwellings. He walks to the end of the crescent-shaped spit and swims across open water to the ice fields off Somerset Island.

THE GATHERING SEASON

Late summer is the golden season of the Far North, between the mosquito swarms of early summer and the cruel cold to come. The days are cool and clear, the nights are dark and crisp. It is a busy season. Those who stay collect food for the winter, or amass fat reserves for hard times. Those who flee, as do most birds, lay on fat to fuel their long flight. ❖ After a short but busy growing season arctic plants {nearly all of them perennials} close down for the long winter. During summer they have hoarded food reserves: sugars, starches and lipids. As winter approaches they store their carbohydrate reserves in roots and rhizomes underground, or in the wintering leaves of evergreens. They also prepare—beneath the soil or at the surface—next year's buds and shoots, often to an advanced stage of development. Thus they go into winter's sleep, ready to jump into rapid growth, to draw on their nutrient reserves the moment warmth and moisture awaken them. ❖ In spring the caribou, among the last of the great wildlife herds left on Earth, begin the migration so vividly described in an Inuit poem:

GLORIOUS IT IS TO SEE
THE CARIBOU FLOCKING DOWN FROM THE FOREST
AND BEGINNING
THEIR WANDERING TO THE NORTH.
GLORIOUS IT IS TO SEE
THE GREAT HERDS FROM THE FOREST
SPREADING OUT OVER PLAINS OF WHITE,
GLORIOUS TO SEE.

They arrive lean and ragged, shedding their dead, bleached winter fur. As they graze all summer and fall on the vast and verdant arctic meadows, they become sleek and bulky, resplendent in their new, clove-brown, short-haired coats. ❖ Once they numbered three million and when these mighty herds marched, Inuit told the explorer Knud Rasmussen, "The whole country is alive and one can see neither the beginning of them nor the end—the whole earth seems to be moving." ❖ In fall the caribou ebb back toward their winter range in the northern forest belt, the final cycle of their two-thousand-mile migration. During the day, the animals scatter, feeding over a vast area. Toward evening, groups coalesce, trickles of animals merging into a great stream. The sun sets over the immense tundra as its lakes reflect the copper sky. The vast throng of migrating caribou flow over the dark earth, a golden ribbon of life in the sun's slanting rays. ❖ The Polar Inuit of northwest Greenland call August, INNANIT AASARNIARTALERFIAT, "the month when the newborn birds fly south." For the parent birds it is a race against time. Every day counts, so their young will be ready to leave the North before the killing frost of fall. There is no time for building an elaborate nest. ❖ For the peregrine falcon the nest is a simple scrape on a cliff ledge used by generations of falcons. Four chicks hatch from the buff-colored, reddish-speckled eggs, little balls of whitish fluff with flesh-colored beaks, and large, awkward feet that will develop deadly talons. The larger female guards them, the smaller male brings food. She takes his catch, tears off tiny pieces and feeds them to chicks that seem

forever hungry. They must grow fast and get on their way, as the peregrine is aptly named "the wanderer." Within a few weeks the eyases must be strong enough to fly thousands of miles to the coastal regions of South America where they will spend the winter. ❖ Before their far-north breeding areas were discovered, snow geese were named CHEN HYPERBOREA by a romantically-inclined ornithologist, "the goose from the lands beyond the north wind." They leave their wintering regions in the southern United States in March and April and arrive at their ancestral summer breeding grounds in May, when snow still covers most of the land. Each goose and gander, mated for life, select a territory, often close to where they nested the previous year, and defend it vehemently against all trespassers. ❖ As soon as snow melt permits, the female lays an average of five eggs. Incubation begins in early June. The goslings, little puffs of golden down, hatch in late June or early July. They leave their down-lined nest within a day, traipse after their large parents, snip tender shoots, eat insects and berries, and grow apace, for time is pressing. They need about forty-five days before they can fly and migrate south with their parents—before the onset of snowstorms and lethal cold. For snow geese with their tight timing, curtailed seasons can be catastrophic. In some years a late spring or early fall fatally shortens their breeding season and there are few goslings among the snow goose flocks that reach the south. ❖ For polar bears the inverse is true. For them a cold spring is a blessing; there is more ice, they can hunt more seals, eat more blubber, lay up more fat reserves.

For the second year in a row, the ice lasts long on Hudson Bay. The female with cubs hunts seals until nearly mid-July. Then a northeast storm breaks and disperses the ice. Mother and cubs are marooned upon a floe and ride with the wind southwest until the waves break their pan into small pieces. The female slides into the water, the cubs follow, swimming towards distant ice. The cubs swim slowly, steadily, in their mother's wake, but after a while, less fat-padded and protected than she, they feel the cold and whine. ❖ The mother makes a shallow dive and comes up beneath the female cub who holds on while her brother quickly clambers aboard. The large female is buoyant; only small wavelets splash her riders. ❖ Sometimes traversing wind-driven ice floes, sometimes swimming, mother and cubs reach the southwest coast of Hudson Bay. A ragged chain of wave-sculpted ice lies in the shallows. The tide is out. The female climbs an ice block, looks carefully around, slides down, and plods across the extensive tidal flats. ❖ The cubs follow reluctantly. Until now they have lived only on pristine ice and snow. They have washed their paws and fur after every meal. Now they wade through dark, oozy mud to shore. The mother stops,

hooks up some kelp with a questing claw, and eats it. The cubs, usually so quick and inquisitive, remain still. When they finally reach shore, their snow-white legs are black. ❖ The family climbs a dune and rests. The cubs lick and gnaw at the drying mud on their paws. Their mother is in a quandary. She would like to follow the coast northward as she did the previous year. Along shore there is always some hope of food: seaweed, small fish trapped in tidal pools, and sometimes a feast: a dead seal, or walrus, or even a whale washed upon the shore. ❖ But there are other bears. After the ice disintegrates, about one thousand polar bears come ashore on the west coast of Hudson Bay. Some travel northward along the shore, searching for food. Most estivate; they dig shallow pits into coastal dunes or lie in the shade of rocky outcrops on islands and doze away the food-poor months of summer, expending a minimum of energy and fat reserves. Since the ice season lasted late into the summer and hunting was good, most bears are fat and non-aggressive. ❖ The female, however, takes no chances. The moment a male pops out of his pit for a curious glance, she "talks" urgently to her cubs. The family backs up and the mother heads inland, as do nearly all other females with cubs.

Adult polar bears communicate mainly by body language. In threat, surprise, or anger they hiss like cornered, furious cats. They chomp and growl and occasionally, in real fury, they roar, a mighty lion-like roar. But generally polar bears are silent. ❖ When strange bears meet they signal peaceful intent and mutual respect by subtle body movements, presumably evaluating by smell and sight each other's size, power, temper, and hierarchical standing. They are careful not to offend, not to provoke. They circle and sniff, a slow-motion polar dance of mutual inspection and classification. If they fear each other, they will part. If one fears the other, he will leave. If they are young males and they like each other they may strike up a friendship that can last for months. As a rule, all these encounters are silent. The bears communicate with each other in mutually intelligible signs. ❖ Polar bear mothers, however, "talk" frequently to their cubs: warnings, commands, deep moans of exasperation, and a nearly humming growl of endearment. The cubs know every nuance of her growls and for the most part, obey promptly.

A much more enticing smell, the dream smell of every polar bear, reaches the great male from Lancaster Sound who walks along the bleak lunar limestone coast of Somerset Island. Perhaps his wanderings are prompted by a vaguely remembered feast of long ago when, as a young and hungry bear, he found a dead whale on this shore in August. Now his superb sense of smell tells him that, further south, another dead whale lies on a beach.

There are three truly arctic whales. The largest is the bowhead whale, its mouth the size of a large living room, its bulging body wrapped in thirty tons of blubber. It was hunted to near extinction by nineteenth-century whalers. ❖ By far the strangest is the narwhal whose single, tapered, spiraled, ivory tusk  is the basis of the many-thousand-year-old unicorn legend. This tusk was once worth, in China, Japan, Arabia, and at the courts of Europe, many times its weight in gold. It was believed to protect its owner from poisoning, a professional hazard of many princes. It was also a symbol of power. The imperial scepters of Austria and Russia are jewel-encrusted narwhal tusks. ❖ The most common arctic whale is the white whale or beluga {a word derived from the Russian BELYI, meaning "white"}. Belugas are gregarious and, fortunately, still numerous—about one-hundred thousand live in the circumpolar northern  seas. They are small, elegant whales. Males are about fifteen feet long and weigh three thousand pounds, females are somewhat smaller and lighter. In summer they cluster in favorite bays, inlets, and estuaries; about one thousand spend three months in the entrance to the Churchill River near the town of Churchill. Several thousand belugas summer in bays of Somerset Island, and about one thousand of them in Cunningham Inlet. ❖ The belugas surge through the cool-green, pellucid water like gleaming ivory-white torpedoes, their heart-shaped flukes rising and falling in smooth cadence, glittering bow waves curling against their heads. Dark-hued calves swim like small shadows near their massive mothers. ❖ The whales come into the bay to molt. When they arrive many are a dull ivory yellow, when they leave most are a glowing Carrara-marble white. Perhaps to hasten the molt, perhaps to scratch an itchy, flaking skin, the whales love to rub and roll upon tide-flooded gravel beaches. Splashing with powerful flukes, they drag one side across the rough bottom, then the other, repeat it on their back, and finally, with a humping motion, undulate their itchy bellies over gravel. ❖ Occasionally they keep it up too long. A safe sport on the rising tide, it can be fatal on the ebb. The water recedes, a whale gets stuck and immediately becomes frantic with fear. It thrashes violently, cries loudly, and tries to hitch and hump its massive body into deeper water.

This year four whales—three adults and a brown-gray immature—are the victim of their play. They dally too long with delightful gravel-scrubbing in Elwin Bay on the east coast of Somerset Island and low tide strands them. At first they splash and scream and then they lie very quiet. It is too late. The initial racket has alerted a young male polar bear sleeping a mile away. He comes immediately to investigate. Though he is only four years old his power is awesome. He quickly kills the four helpless whales and feasts to utter repletion. ❖ The high tide pushes the whale carcasses higher up the beach. Their smell spreads. Each breeze broadcasts the promise of food, and bears far away rise, sniff, decode and begin to march towards the promised banquet. ❖ The second bear to arrive is another young male. He is cautious but not nervous. The two bears circle each other, the sated bear goes back to sleep, and the newcomer feeds. ❖ Next is a big bear. Despite the fact that he is much larger than the two young males with the whales, and more than twice as heavy, the big male advances slowly, circumspectly. In polar bear society, prior presence at a source of food seems to confer some rights. Thrusting out his lower lip, the great male sig-

nals peace and goodwill. Partly reassured, the two young males move aside, and the big bear begins to eat. ❖ By the time the large bear from Lancaster Sound arrives, the whales have been dead for ten days and have attracted five bears. Of them all, the male with the chevron scar is by far the most powerful. He has walked for many days and has eaten noth-ing for a long time. ❖ He gradually approaches and the four other bears immediately rise, alarmed by his size and power. The great bear signals nonaggression and sidles toward the dead whales. There is plenty of food for all. He tears off chunks of skin and blubber and eats steadily for more than an hour and finally he is full. ❖ His stomach bulges with more than a hundred pounds of blubber. He walks to the sea edge, washes his paws and muzzle, ambles to a gravel bench, and slumps. Full and tired, he rests his great triangular head upon folded front paws, and falls asleep.

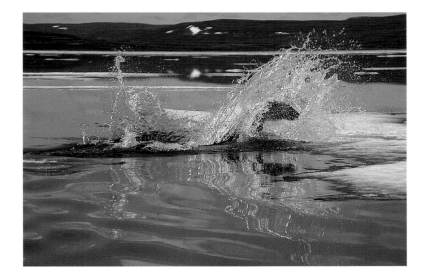

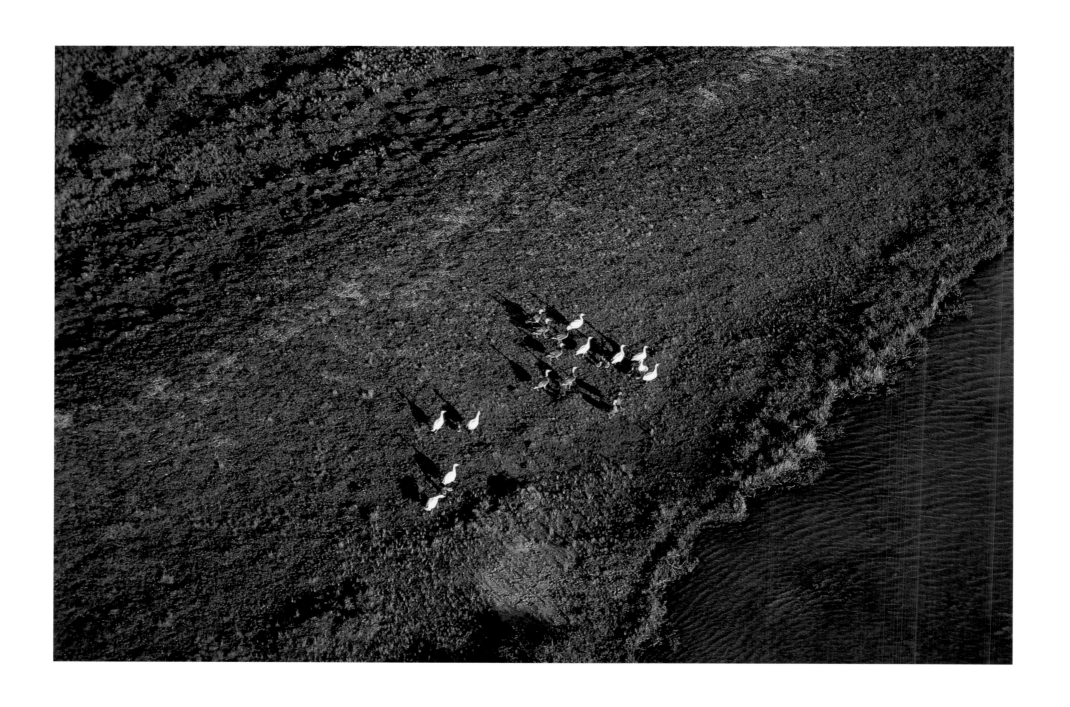

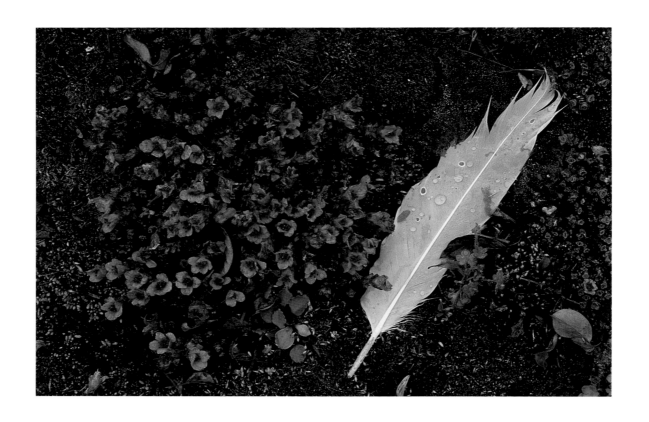

WAITING FOR WINTER

Polar bears are perhaps the only creatures in the Arctic that truly long for winter. For plants, insects, birds and mammals summer, however brief, is a season of birth and growth and plenty. For the polar bear, summer is a time of fasting and, often, intolerable heat. ❖ Polar bears are essentially bears of the ice, rightly called "ice bears" in many languages {ISBJØRN in Danish; IJSBEER in Dutch; EISBÄR in German}. Their ancestor is the now-extinct cave bear of Eurasia. This huge animal that measured eight to nine feet long and weighed about fifteen hundred pounds inspired both fear and awe in early man. He both hunted and worshipped it. ❖ Deep in the Drachenloch {the Dragon's Lair}, a fear-haunted cave in Switzerland, the archaeologist Emil Bächler found an altar-like stone slab, erected by Neanderthal men perhaps fifty thousand or more years ago. According to the famous scholar Joseph Campbell, the slab was placed here "for the ritual of the bear—the earliest altars of any kind yet found, or known of, anywhere in the world." Arranged upon it were seven bear skulls, all facing the entrance of the cave. The great bear was man's first god and, like an echo from the dawn of man, the cultic killing and veneration of the bear by most circumpolar people has persisted nearly to our day. ❖ A cousin and contemporary of the cave bear developed into today's brown bear. The grizzly of Eurasia and America is predominantly vegetarian, but will gladly eat anything available—salmon, ground squirrels, caribou calves, carrion, even garbage. It consumes prodigious amounts of food in summer, grows very fat in fall, and avoids the unpleasantness of winter by hibernating. ❖ Some 200,000 years ago during a particularly cold period of the Pleistocene, mile-thick ice sheets spread and covered much of Europe. Seas as far south as France and Spain were covered by ice in winter. Seals were common and tame, they had no enemies, and basked blissfully upon the ice without a fear or worry. ❖ As the enterprising brown bears discovered this food source, they ventured out onto the ice. In a remarkably short time, on the evolutionary scale, the brown bears of this area evolved into white-furred, ice-loving, seal-eating polar bears. The ice fields then extended far to the south and so did the first polar bears. The oldest known polar bear fossil {a 100,000-year-old leg bone} was discovered near the Kew Bridge in London. ❖ This parallels, in many ways, the evolution of the Inuit. Their ancestors came out of Asia, where they hunted land mammals; reindeer, mainly, and mammoth before these arctic giants became extinct. They crossed the Bering Strait about eight thousand years ago and settled in the vacant lands of the Arctic. ❖ At first these people hunted arctic land mammals: caribou and muskoxen. Slowly they acquired the skills and invented the tools for successful sea mammal hunting until they finally, like polar bears, adapted to the Arctic life. ❖ After the last ice age peak eighteen thousand years ago, the glaciers and ice fields receded and arctic seals and polar bears retreated with the waning ice to the remote and

mysterious north. Marco Polo reported in the thirteenth century that the Chinese knew the "Region of Darkness" was inhabited by "bears of a white color, and of prodigious size..."

The female and her two cubs walk inland, two to six miles from the coast, far enough away from the potentially dangerous male bears. It is a land of meadows and marshes, of willow thickets and, upon drier ground, small copses of tightly clustered spruces. In summer this region is aswarm with mosquitoes. On calm days they fill the air with a humming haze and drive man and beast to frenzy. Now the frosts of fall have finished them. ❖ The berries are ripe: blue bilberries, juicy and sweet; black, shiny crowberries, watery and sourish; and amber-yellow cloudberries. Unlike grizzlies that rake berries methodically with blunt, finger-long, iron-hard claws and munch them by the bushel, the female polar bear with her short, sharp, nearly cat-like claws is an awkward berry picker. Where berries grow thick, she scratches them together and eats them. The cubs copy her and soon their muzzles and bums are berry blue. ❖ The bear family is surrounded by more expert berry pickers. Everywhere ptarmigan are harvesting this bounty of fall. The female bear ignores them. She is wise to the ways of birds: just as you think you have them, they fly away. But the rustling and running of ptarmigan through the golden-yellow grass of fall fascinates the cubs and incites their hunting instincts. They crash after ptarmigan and stop, startled, as the birds fly up with a hard clatter of wings and land farther away. It keeps the cubs busy and does the ptarmigan no harm. If the cubs stray too far, their mother's deep growl brings them hurriedly back to her.

In this region rich in willows and dwarf birch, ptarmigan are common. They change color to match the seasons: pure white in winter, they are piebald in spring; part winter's white, part summer's brown. In summer they are a rich, earthy brown touched with gray; a perfect camouflage. Now, in fall, they change again to match the coming snow. They also grow snowshoes, a dense layer of feathers both upon their feet and underneath them, to walk upon soft snow. They snip the carbohydrate-rich willow buds, their main winter food, at an average rate of thirty-five buds per minute—according to a study by a patient scientist— or more than two thousand buds per hour. ❖ During July and August, the male bears along the coast and the females with cubs further inland ate little and slept a lot. Now, in September, they begin to stir. There is a feel of coming winter. The nights are dark and cold. Black ice with silvery bubbles and veins glazes the

smaller tundra ponds. In the morning, each waxy, wine-red bearberry leaf is rimmed with a filigree of delicate crystals. ❖ The few summer birds that remain are gripped by a febrile restlessness. Nervous, twittering flocks of snow buntings drift like snowflakes across the land. Late-traveling sandpipers probe the mud that rims ponds and lakes, leaving patterns of three-toed tracks among those of passing caribou. Oldsquaw ducks gather in excited gabby rafts upon a lake and talk about cold and migration. High in the sky, skeins of snow geese wing toward the south. The roughly one thousand polar bears scattered along hundreds of miles of Hudson Bay coast feel the same restlessness, but they do not rush. ❖ Now most of the bears begin a slow, uncoordinated, seemingly haphazard northward drift. They swim across the Nelson River and cluster at favorite capes where ancient knowledge tells them the Hudson Bay freeze-up will begin, allowing them to leave the land of hunger for the frozen sea and seals. By mid-October about eight hundred bears are massed along the hundred-mile coastal stretch between the Nelson River in the south and the Churchill River in the north. It is the greatest concentration of polar bears in the world. ❖ Although many polar bears move along the coast, they have little contact. Large bears regally ignore each other and all other bears. Small bears deem it prudent to avoid large bears, although there is no real danger, for small scared bears can run much faster {top speed is thirty-five miles per hour} than the massive males. But medium-sized bears, young males from four to eight years old weighing three to seven hundred pounds, may form friendships and then travel and play together. ❖ A young male, five years old and nicely padded with fat, wanders north along the Hudson Bay coast in that deceptively absent-minded shamble that hides alertness and latent power. The north wind has told him that somewhere ahead is another bear but, as yet, he cannot see him. He approaches slowly, carefully. The other bear, a male of roughly equal size and age, half hidden by a boulder, is suddenly aware of the new bear and rises abruptly. They face each other, apprehensive, careful not to give offense. Both signal "peace." They circle and sniff. By smell and minute movements they evaluate each other and convey respect and friendly interest. They come closer and closer and finally stop, face each other, stretch their sinuous necks, and touch noses. First encounters between such bears tend to be courteous but very cautious. ❖ With jaws wide open they "mouth" each other or gently nibble each other's necks. One places a massive, fur-fringed paw upon the other's shoulder, they rise and spar and push, lose balance and embrace, sway and wrestle. One topples and lies on his back, huge paws pedaling in the air. The other, jaws agape, throws himself on top. It looks ferocious, but in fact both bears are very careful, very gentle, like two gigantic shaggy puppies having a marvelous romp. For the next two months they are inseparable. They travel and even sleep together, and when the mood is right, they play.

The female and her cubs also march slowly northward, slightly inland to avoid the males on the coast. They pass the area where, nine months ago, the cubs were born and where in March they rode through deep snow on their mother's back to the ice of Hudson Bay. ❖ By late September the family has reached the region five miles inland from Cape Churchill where the male bears begin to gather. The wind veers to the northeast and brings with it the first snowstorm of the season. Mother and cubs seek shelter from the wind-lashed snow in the lee of a willow thicket. The cubs cuddle close against their mother's protective body and slowly a thick layer of snow covers them. The snowstorm, with vicious gusts to seventy miles per hour, lasts a night, a day, and another night. The bears sleep peacefully beneath their blanket of snow. ❖ The storm ends and the sun rises, a pale-orange disk over a land infinitely still and serene. A faint roseate blush suffuses the air and delicately tints the tracery of snow upon willows and spruces. In this pearly Monet light, a lump of snow begins to stir. Mother and cubs wake up and shake themselves. They are itchy after their long rest. They roll and rub in the snow, twisting and turning with pleasure, great paws wagging limply in the air. The female turns, digs a shallow pit into the new-fallen snow, and settles back. Her cubs snuggle eagerly against her reclining body and begin to nurse.

THE COVERING ICE

In the high Arctic, winter begins once again. The sun sets in mid-October and will not rise again until mid-February. It is a pallid world, a world of grays and blacks and velvety blues and glints of milky moon-light upon the ice. In this phantasmagoric world of shifting shapes and shadows, this world without depth and distance, legends and lore of the Inuit assume new meaning. Their fears and ghosts become real, for these spirits were born in the blue-gray gloom of the arctic night. ❖ New ice covers the sea—thin, dark, and treacherous. It is at this time that the most courageous and experienced Polar Inuit begin their winter seal hunt, the "smooth-ice hunt," the most dangerous hunt of all. Over their regular double-layered sealskin boots they slip on large overshoes made of polar bear fur and, armed with harpoon and gun, slide out upon the smooth, elastic, yielding ice. If a hunter makes one mistake and breaks through, he is doomed. His frantic fingers find no hold upon the glass-smooth ice, cold quickly paralyzes him, his struggles become feebler, and in ten minutes he dies. ❖ While slowly-freezing sea ice has a salinity of about two parts per mill, this fast-frozen sea ice of early winter may carry twenty. Increased salinity gives ice greater

tensile strength and this ice has about twice the tensile strength of freshwater ice equally thick. ❖ The hunter slides soundlessly across the ice in a peculiar, broad-legged shuffle that distributes his weight. The ice bends like rubber. In the gloom, the hunter listens intently for the telltale snorting gurgle, the deep breathing of a surfacing seal. He slides to the newly formed aglu and waits, still and alert. The seal surfaces again and with lightning speed the hunter harpoons and shoots nearly simultaneously. With utmost caution he hauls the carcass onto the thin ice. This is his first seal of the season.

The great bear at Elwin Bay has had a relaxed and food-filled summer and fall thanks to the four beached beluga whales. By late fall only bones, fat-coated pebbles and dirty bears remain. Rancid oil stains the bear's fur a dark amber that no amount of washing in cold sea water will remove. ❖ Now the great bear moves cautiously out onto the newly-formed ice. If he were to fall into the water, the splash would warn all seals for miles around. He slides across the smooth ice, nearly spread-eagled to distribute his great weight, and smells and listens for the scent and sound of seals. ❖ He glides with utmost caution to the edge of a newly-formed breathing hole and waits, half-crouched, tense and alert. The seal surfaces and in an instant, the bear grabs it, kills it, and hauls it carefully onto the thin ice. This is his first seal of the season.

Polar bears gather at Cape Churchill, more than one thousand miles south of Lancaster Sound, though ice will not form there for another month or two. At first, all are males. ❖ A broad, pebble-covered esker meanders across the cape from east to west, flanked on the north by shallow lagoons and on the south by marshy tundra ponds hemmed with willow thickets. The cape ends in a crescentic, boulder-strewn spur that hooks out into the dark waters of Hudson Bay. Just beyond its tip is a tiny island. As many as thirty polar bears gather on this islet, sleeping near the east edge, close to the sea. ❖ Cape Churchill has long been known as a trysting place of polar bears. The British explorer David Hanbury camped ten days at Cape Churchill because "polar bears were said to be numerous there." The Hudson's Bay Company surveyor and explorer Peter Fidler rounded the cape by canoe on August 22, 1807, and "saw 5 White Bears upon" the tiny island near its tip. Now, in October and November, two to three hundred polar bears may be in the vicinity of Cape Churchill, and up to seventy at the cape itself. ❖ Polar bears are supposedly solitary creatures that roam the vastness of the north. Male bears, said the explorer and writer Peter Freuchen, are among "the loneliest creatures on Earth....they always keep some distance apart and never

approach each other." Thor Larsen, for a long time Norway's top polar bear specialist, agreed—"When polar bears occasionally meet on the ice or on the tundra they will pass each other at a distance of fifty to one hundred meters or more." ❖ At the cape, the bears coexist in reasonable peace and harmony based largely on respect for hierarchy. The first bears arrive in late September, and settle in to sleep and wait. A newcomer approaches the cape's resident bears with circumspection. He walks slowly and deliberately towards them, pausing frequently, head high, sniffing and weaving slightly from side to side. He may rise on his hind feet for a better look, but he relies primarily on his acute sense of smell to identify and classify the resident bears. In turn, they assess his size, intent, and social standing. ❖ If he is small- or medium-sized, the local bears pay little heed. But if he is large, eight-hundred pounds or more, his appearance causes a stir. Young bears become apprehensive and may trot away, and old, decrepit bears become huffy and defensive. They rise and growl and hiss, upper lips puffed out, hairs raised on necks and along curved, protruding spines. The newcomer, no matter how powerful, will nearly always back away from a hostile bear. He has come to await the forming of the ice, to eat kelp, perhaps to sleep, but not to fight. ❖ This year the king  of the cape is a mighty bear, weighing twelve hundred pounds or more, all muscle and superiority. His arrival causes a commotion. All bears get up. A few are hostile. Most are careful and humble. The stately bear ignores them. He walks with the slow majesty of absolute power. Evidently he knows the cape, for he heads directly to a small bay where high tides have amassed thick layers of kelp that, because of anaerobic fermentation, have the sour smell of silage. The bears love it; they might as well for there is little else to eat at the cape. A few bears who are feeding bow away respectfully as the mighty bear approaches; he starts to dig up kelp and eat it. ❖ On the lowest rung of the hierarchical ladder are the very young bears. They are understandably nervous and jumpy. Until recently, they had a mighty mother to protect them. When in trouble, they only had to yell and she rushed to the rescue. Now they are alone. Wisely, most are cautious, timid, and quick to run. But a few little males, hungry, cocky and aggressive, will charge a bear five times their weight to get food. ❖ Often they get away with it, perhaps because it is such a drastic breach of polar bear etiquette and takes the larger bear by surprise. Eventually, though, these little toughs run into bigger toughs, and are hurt or at least badly scared. Both the young and the great avoid the bad-tempered, very old bears. They have a private sphere that none may transgress, lunging with hardly any warning at bears that come too near. ❖ This year there are many bears at the cape. One is particularly foul-tempered. This bear is hostile and aggressive—all the bears are ill-at-ease when he is near. Most old bears no longer play-fight. Like certain people, they appear bent, grouchy, and arthritic. Only fear or the prospect of food rouses them. ❖ And then there are the bears that play. Young males engage in play-fight behavior that is as ritualized and stylized as a medieval jousting match. Despite their awesome power, they take great care not to hurt each other. ❖ Bears that play together are of roughly equal size, age, and weight. Young bears, the recently abandoned two- or three-year-olds, rarely play. They are usually hungry and scared and have no fat reserves to fuel the activity. ❖ At times a large male in the mood for play approaches a little bear, but the invitation is rarely taken up. The large bear advances slowly and hunches down low, signaling peace with every nuance of posture and movement in the complex and subtle text of ursine body language. The little bear, apprehensive and abristle, keeps backing up; both wander around the cape, one forward and one backward, until the small bear wheels and flees. ❖ On rare occasions the gentleness of the large bear will allay the small bear's fears and they will carefully play together. In such unequal play-fights initiated by a large bear, the little bear nearly always "wins." The large one, powerful enough to injure his small opponent severely with one swat, uses utmost caution and restraint not to intimidate the little fellow, because that would instantly end the fight and the fun. So he lets himself be pummeled and pushed by the small bear and frequently goes limp and collapses. ❖ Some playmates arrive together at the cape. These are the bears that have established a friendship bond while traveling north-ward along the coast of Hudson Bay. Others meet at the cape, become friends, and play together. Bears that play together usually stay together. They feed next to each other, remain together until ice forms, and leave the cape together. These friendships may last even longer, for bears in pairs are seen weeks after freeze-up on the ice of Hudson Bay. ❖ Much more amazing, and unique, are the friendships between certain polar bears and sled dogs. The huskies belong to Brian Ladoon, a native of Churchill. He tethers his two teams of magnificent huskies on long chains near the coast of Hudson Bay, about ten miles east of Churchill. Polar bears pass frequently in late fall and early winter, stop and investigate, attracted by the smell of the dogs' food. But the yelping, howling, and screaming of the dogs {like wolves, true huskies do not bark} usually scares them away. ❖ In fall of 1992, something strange happened. A large male bear wandered close, unworried by the frantic dogs, lay down and waited. Eventually the dogs simmered down. The bear moved closer and picked the husky that seemed least hostile. The dog weighed sixty pounds, the bear more than seven hundred. While all the other huskies howled in a frenzy of excitement, this dog and bear became friends—the dog cautious, careful, apprehensive at first, the bear gentle, slow, appeasing. The bear returned each day and soon bear and dog were romping and playing. The bear had this one special friend, but he also made friends with several other huskies. The rest of the tethered dogs were either neutral or hostile, and those he ignored. ❖ The body language of dog and bear are totally different. A friendly dog wags his tail. The round-rumped polar bear has no tail to wag and does not understand this signal. The bear's thrust-out lower lip, meaning "I am friendly," means nothing to the dog. ❖ But just as language barriers among humans can be overcome by people of good will, bear and dog manage to

convey their affection for each other. The dog rubs against the bear and licks it fondly, the bear pets his slender friend with a huge, furry paw. And then they play; the dog exuberant and excited, jumping, running, and the bear rolling, hugging, swatting, using caution not to hurt his companion. Finally, hot and exhausted, they lie down together and sleep. ❖ As it grows colder and lakes and lagoons freeze, the lure of the cape becomes stronger. Ice will form first near the cape. Ice means release from the hungry land and the promise of fat seals after months of fasting. The bears cluster at the cape and wait and hope to return as soon as possible to their true home, the frozen sea.

The female with cubs approaches the cape from the north, upwind from the male bears. Suddenly she smells something and rushes ahead. A snowy owl has killed an eider duck and is just beginning to eat it. The owl sees the rushing bear, and tries to lift off with its kill. But the duck is heavy, and the bear fast. The owl drops its prey, rises silently on broad, rounded wings, lands on a snow-covered driftwood log and, with glowing yellow eyes, watches the bear eat its duck. ❖ Since she came ashore in July the female, who is nursing two rapidly growing cubs, has eaten only grasses, berries, kelp, and a few lemmings and voles—poor fare for a big bear. Despite her hunger, she eats the duck with fastidious slowness. The male cub slides towards his mother on his furry belly, all innocence and guile. The mother ignores him. She looks up to make sure that all is well, and in that instant, the little male snitches the last piece of duck and trots off. ❖ At the cape, the female keeps a cautious distance from the males. She is constantly alert and picks places to rest where she cannot be surprised by a prowling male. This year her precautions are not necessary. Nearly all bears are still fat and placid. In other years, when the bears are lean and hungry, the cape can be an exceedingly dangerous place for a female bear with young cubs. ❖ The mother rests, her cubs play. Sometimes they roughhouse—the young male's idea of fun is to half-strangle his sister. They play with each other and sometimes they invent games. Today brother and sister are busily tunneling from opposite sides into a wind-formed snow ridge. Finally they pierce the ridge, one squeezes through the tunnel and challenges the "enemy" on the other side. They slide back and forth through their tunnel. Finally the young male climbs on top of the snow ridge and with that stiff-legged pile-driver pounce adult bears use to break into seal nunarjaks, he collapses the tunnel. ❖ The mother pulls out lymegrass and eats the starchy roots and rhizomes. The cubs imitate her. One cub digs straight down into deep snow until only a small round rump can be seen.

Days and nights are cold and clear. The sea is cooling rapidly. Crystals of freshwater ice begin to form. They grow, link with other crystals, and enclose within themselves minute pockets of salt water. The sea, now filled with a thick layer of ice crystals, becomes heavy, sluggish; gray swells lap slowly over coastal rocks and coat them with ice. This is called frazil ice or, less elegantly, slob ice. ❖ Finally it is nearly gruel-thick; a gull can land and stand on it. On a very cold, still night the ice crystals coagulate and form a firm, thin sheet of elastic new ice called nilas. As yet, it is only coastal ice. The next day is cloudy and the sky is a dull lead-black, the "water sky" of arctic sailors, the reflection of dark open water upon the clouds. Its opposite is "iceblink," the yellowish or whitish light on clouds reflected by distant ice fields. ❖ Now comes the most annoying, tantalizing time for the land-bound bears at the cape. Just when the ice is strong enough to leave the land, the wind changes, a storm rages over cape and sea, breaks up the newly-formed ice, and drives the brash-ice far out into Hudson Bay. ❖ New ice forms along the coast, the wind veers, the broken ice returns, and a jumble of new ice and ice pans lay piled against the cape, moving to and fro with the tides and leaving pools of jade-green water near shore, hemmed by milk-white ice. The bears try to walk out, fall in, jump from pan to pan, are carried out on the ebb, and return, disgruntled with the flood. ❖ Near the end of November the weather, so gusty and shifting for a week, changes. The temperature drops to minus-thirty and even minus-forty degrees Fahrenheit. It is still and cutting cold. The shifting floes coalesce; at last the sea freezes far out into Hudson Bay. The bears move. Every day there are fewer bears at the cape—the moment they have waited for all these months has finally arrived.

Among the last to leave is the female with her cubs. She walks ahead, carefully picking a path through the tide-heaved ice sheets. The cubs follow her closely. Slowly they vanish in the distance, faint yellow forms upon the vastness of the ice, their true realm.

Polar Dance was produced by Images of Nature®

Design by Lee Carlman Riddell

Text Edited by Cara Blessley

Map and polar bear drawings by Mike Reagan

The text was set in bitstream calligraphic 421 and 810 italic, and adobe zapf dingbats

Production coordination by Steven Goff

Printing was done in Hong Kong through Palace Press International, San Francisco

The book was printed in five colors on mitsubishi matte artpaper 157 gsm

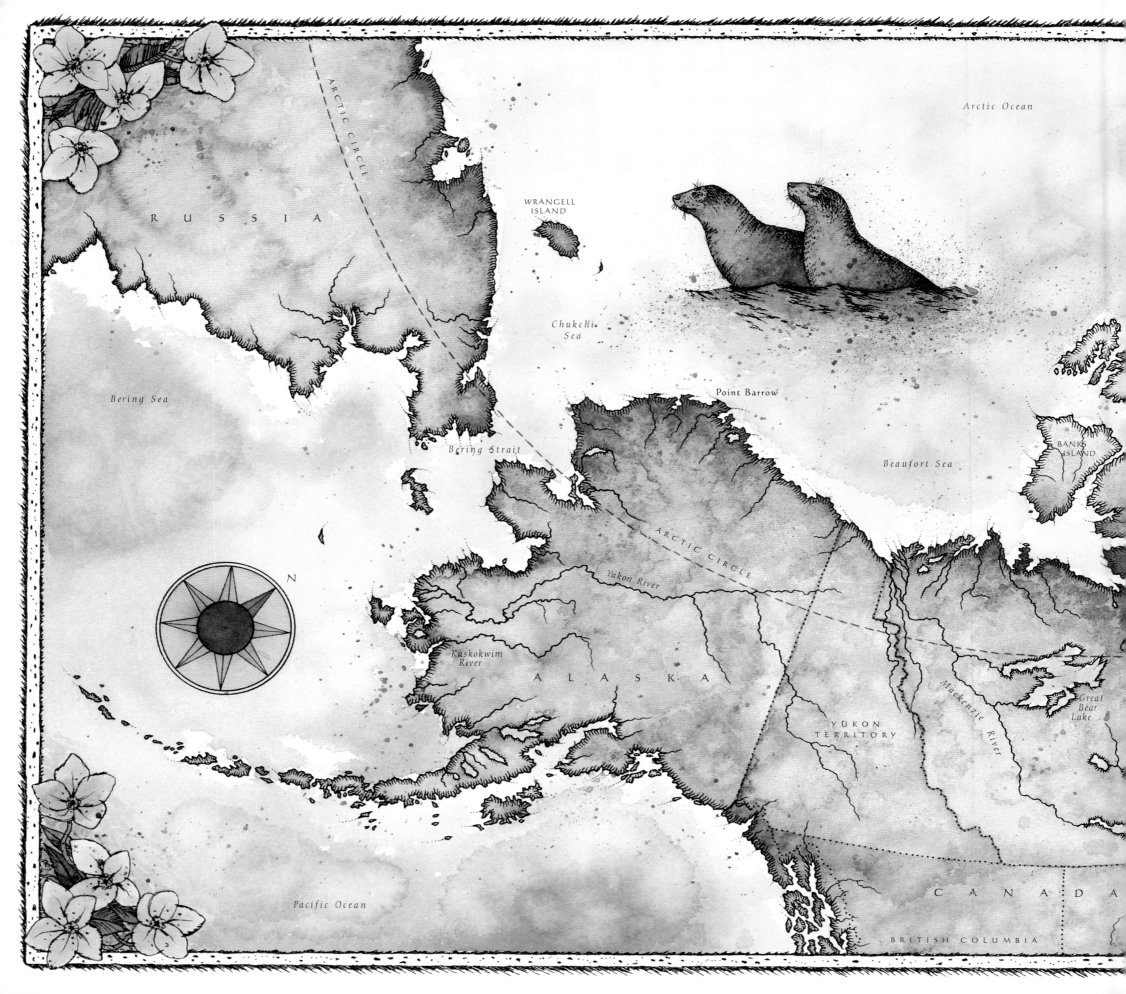

RUSSIA

Arctic Ocean

WRANGELL
ISLAND

*Chukchi
Sea*

Point Barrow

Bering Sea

Beaufort Sea

BANKS
ISLAND

Bering Strait

ARCTIC CIRCLE

Yukon River

N

*Kuskokwim
River*

A L A S K A

YUKON
TERRITORY

Mackenzie River

*Great
Bear
Lake*

Pacific Ocean

C A N A D A

BRITISH COLUMBIA